PRAISE FOR, *YOU WI*
UNIQUELY HELPFUL GUIDEBOOK)

"Aside from editing, I really enjoyed reading your manuscript. I've had my own personal troubles this past year, so much of what you wrote really spoke to me. Thank you"

-Teah, Oregon

"I have never had a book impact me as this one has. Dannie's openness, sincerity, and honesty about what others may not want to discuss from their own lives is the key that opens the reader's personal involvement quietly and intimately, and then creates an understanding of being able to overcome great difficulties.

Not everyone will have had to climb so far, but everyone will understand that the possibilities of doing so are within them and can be found in their own lives to begin that change that will be absolutely mind boggling.

Reading is the first step, realizing is the second, and the third is the recovery of possibilities. This is one great book!"

-Arn, Florida

"To truly be successful in life, you have to put the negative events from the past behind you and take responsibility for your own life.

You Will Be Ok, I Promise, explores pathways to recovery and success. The author - Dannie Duncan - tells her story honestly and with a sense of humor. She can laugh at herself, which really helps to put life into perspective.

I recommend this book to anyone who is in need of relief from the challenges of life!"

-RJ, Oregon

"Chapter seven about your encounter with Ida Duke really made me believe in the magic of life again - thank you!

-Shari, Georgia

Dannie Duncan

"Jealousy occurs when you bond with another person because of your lack of wholeness and right relationship to self and God. You then struggle with a known or unknown competitor." [1]

The hidden wisdom – *"The spiritual attitude is to state your preference in your relationship and surrender it to God. If it is meant to be, it will happen; if not, it was not meant to be."* [1]

– Joshua David Stone, PH.D

<u>YOU WILL BE OK, I PROMISE!</u>
(A Uniquely Helpful Guidebook)

DANNIE DUNCAN

BOOK COVER ILLUSTRATION BY MELISSA DUNCAN

BACK COVER BY ROBERT DUNCAN

FUNDS FINDER & CO LLC

..*

"Many people who suffer with hypochondriasis just need some attention."(1)

The hidden wisdom – "Give yourself permission to ask for what you need." (1)

– Lucinda Bassett

<>*<>*<>*<>*

"If you have been faithful to your ideal, you will hear the call when circumstances are ready to materialize your plans and results will correspond in the exact ratio of your fidelity to your ideal."[1]

The hidden wisdom – *"The ideal steadily held is what predetermines and attracts the necessary conditions for its fulfillment."* [1]

– **Charles F. Haanel**

DEDICATION

This book is dedicated to:

The Hero or Heroine in You!

$*_**_**$

"To me, true prosperity begins with feeling good about yourself. It is also the freedom to do what you want to do, when you want to do it. " (1)

The hidden wisdom – *"It is never an amount of money; it is a state of mind. Prosperity or lack of it is an outer expression of the ideas in your head."* (1)

– Louise L. Hay

***

CONTENTS

******

***

I'D LIKE TO THANK

*My great teachers whose works I've quoted throughout this guidebook. You shared your wisdom with the world, and your teachings pulled me back from the edge; I am forever grateful!

*My late mother for buying me flowers every week, which nurtured my healing; thank you - until we meet again!

*My son "sun."

*My cousin - my teacher and spiritual mirror.

*My husband, thank you for giving me my love story.

******

Dannie Duncan

***

Note from the Author -

<u>S</u>mile <u>A</u>nd <u>G</u>rief <u>E</u>vaporates!

If you have been deeply hurt on any level, you may feel like you will never be the same again. Smiling feels foreign to you, and you may notice that you are attracting negative people like flies to a sweat shop.

I invite you to please read on. There are secrets enclosed, that will help you sleep again, smile again, feel comfortable in your own skin again, think positively again, laugh again, love again; you will be OK - I promise - from my heart to yours.

******

***

Foreword

Dear Reader,

When I read this book, I see more and more layers to consider, and since I work with people who are attempting change, I see in this little book a new insight, something that may click with you on one of the many levels stirred up within us as we read about someone else's personal triumphs over unimaginable odds and admissions of errors along the way. Who hasn't made many mistakes? Dannie makes this journey seem easier than it was, and her intent is to make it easier for you than it was for her. I believe she succeeds.

She balances her experiences, many quite difficult and destructive, with her working toward a different experience. Perhaps being guided, she recognizes that other options exist, that bring much more peace and assurance of right choices. She believes, as I do, that nobody deserves bad treatment. Nobody!

She then balances her personal experience and growth with supportive and constructive lessons from some great people who have worked to help others and definitely helped her.

And, she puts it all together in a very readable way, a way that permits either very short reading sessions or long and contemplative ones. Surely you will contemplate using either method.

I'd like to write a brief letter to you, the reader, that I believe may address stumbling blocks that each of us has experienced on our personal journeys toward hope for an improved tomorrow. One error - or multiple mistakes - does not need to stop us from keeping on. When we realize how many people have overcome horrible odds, we might realize that WE CAN, TOO. These are called choices, but choices bring support with them, whether good or bad. We can make better choices.

Arn

A short letter to you:

Hummm, OK, you forgot the poem, Grandma's advice, something a good friend said when you might have used it. You feel as if you have failed again.

That is not true. What it means is that you DID start on the journey of "all the way." Any play on the roulette wheel of life will bring consequences, and sometimes the consequences are that you need to start again, remember again, take a chance again, and then, surely enough, when taking the new chance, the difficulties will reappear, guaranteed.

However, each time we procrastinate on learning, the next test gets a bit harder. So, we must prove to ourselves that we can go all the way. It takes guts, determination, fear, stepping forward, meeting failure, hiding, and retrying. Finally, after making the little baby steps all along so far, we take a stride, maybe hide it, then we move forward through all of the shit once more.

But at that time, the feeling is right and the hiding no longer feels right, until finally, you say, "To hell with it. This is who I am! Take it or leave it, this is who I am. I am doing this, and it feels right, and I am satisfied while hungry, happy while sad, and bothered by the baggage I carry with me. At that point, although life remains far from perfect, as it is life after all, YOU will know that the journey has been the right one, and you will feel success no matter the situation. So many of the parables will become real. The philosophers will make sense. The basics will be the core. And, you will know.

Somehow after wandering around, and you still may be wandering around, you will still know. Then, let the ball fall where it may. Let the roulette wheel be spun again, but you will NOT NEED to play. You will play because you KNOW in spite of your discomfort. You will know when others need to be set free; you will know when your path has shifted enough that the old has passed away with little remorse on your part. You will know.

You will know that your life has changed, and the anchors of the past have been cut away with no trepidation but with determination - and no more lifting of the heavy weight.

This may not be easy. It may take some time. But, a big but, once started, your life will never be the same. You will grow in strength and determination, and you will succeed in becoming the real YOU inside. The sooner you start, the sooner the old all goes away – not without some mishaps, but it goes away.

We must remember that life is never without problems, but it is the way we face them that is important.

OK, now read the book, get started, understand, investigate around you and inside you, and know that each of these things is putting you on the path toward a better life from which there are better things to choose. This book can let your journey make more sense, and it allows you to know that you are not alone on the path.

Arn

<><<<*

Arn is a Public Speaker and Expert Questioner. His team strongly believes that old systems will no longer work, and that greater success comes to any organization - large or small, corporate, public or private, political or non-political - when the people directly involved are valued and listened to.

Thus, <u>Leading From The Bottom Up</u> becomes a new and valid way of working for positive changes in our daily lives.

Playing with new rules shakes life up and makes for an exciting and productive work place, happier living, and a better world.

"It is in rethinking that we change our lives. Each person has the ability to do so. This is a minimum value that can be appreciated individually or in large groups of people. Identifying core values as a group becomes not only worthwhile but also invigorating, leading individuals within the group to achieve their highest possible results, that they can easily find within themselves."

Contact Arn by emailing to – arnlead001@gmail.com

******

Introduction

If you are under duress, you have the right to explore silence. If you give up the right to explore silence, remember that all of your thoughts, words, and deeds will be held for or against you in a court of universal law.

You have the right to the highest divine council. If you choose not to acknowledge or believe in the highest divine council, guides and angels have been - and always will be - assigned to assist you.

But for the former, you must listen to the faint voices within, and for the latter, you must ask them first, because in most cases they need your permission to intervene. Do you understand these rights as they are so stated?

* * * * * *

A seer once told me that I'd spent the first half of my life learning lessons and the second half of my life applying the lessons I'd learned.

The hidden wisdom - *don't wait until the second half of your life to apply life lessons, apply them as you go!*

I DARK NIGHT OF THE SOUL

As I peered out the window at the morning, I viewed it like an unwelcome guest, imagining that it would trip on the steps as it departed toward afternoon. Life was tiresome, and my hope for the future played a competitive game of chess with bleak reality. Sanity was slow dancing with its morbid shadow.

Fear was my confidant.

Feeling like exposed road-kill on a hot desert highway, vultures circled overhead, and I watched dispassionately as they took turns gnawing away at my body. My skin and muscles hurt, and raw nerves shifted daily. Without, things bled together, and the only thing within was the overwhelming compulsion to crawl out of my own skin.

Was I experiencing the after-effects of a nervous breakdown??

I didn't know, but it didn't matter – nothing mattered. Life's sizzle and sparkle were gone, and if anyone attempted to draw me out of myself, my mind rebelled. All I knew was that if I were to survive this utterly retched pain, I had to walk through it; there was no going around it.

The road back to a normal life was long and arduous. It took years of healing to restore my basic health and feel balance again. I learned an assortment of therapeutic secrets along the way, and then as time passed by, something interesting happened.

Whenever I opened my mouth I was compelled to speak my truth to whom-ever would receive it. Small talk or idle chatter became hard to engage in, and it literally hurt me to converse with phony people who put on airs. If I did, it felt like an excruciating waste of my time. I found it to be almost intolerable to live in an inauthentic way.

The Collins English Dictionary defines a nervous breakdown as: "... any mental illness not primarily of organic origin in which the patient ceases to function properly, often accompanied by severely impaired concentration, anxiety, insomnia, and lack of self-esteem; used esp. of episodes of depression."[1] The phrase "nervous breakdown" is not recognized by professionals as a condition in and of itself. It is an umbrella term for any number of diagnosable mental or emotional disorders that interfere with normal behavioral function.

"Dark Night of the Soul" is another non-medical term often used to describe this kind of life-crisis.

Whatever you want to call it, if you live through any kind of life-trauma, you'll come out on the other end altered for better or worse depending on your resolve. In any case, it can take quite a long time to feel balanced and healthy again.

The clinical terms for what I was diagnosed with by medical professionals were Generalized Anxiety Disorder, Social-Phobia, Panic Disorder, and Dysthymia - a low-grade chronic depression. I had developed allergies to dust, cats, and grass. My adrenal glands were burnt out, my hormones were out of balance, and I had developed a lactose and a gluten intolerance as well.

The results were problems with headaches, sinus infections with nose-bleeds, extreme fatigue and dizziness, insomnia, chronic neck and shoulder pain, paranoia, stomach aches, hives, eczema, bursitis, mood swings, periodic bouts of self-induced isolation, ruminating negative thoughts, deep sadness, and - the worst symptom - "around the clock panic attacks." There were compulsions present to drink alcohol, have sex, eat junk food, people-please, and apologize.

I didn't end up in a hospital, but I did have to quit my jobs, sell everything I owned, and board a plane. I flew across the country from Oregon to Georgia to move back in with my mother until I could re-establish at least minimal health on every level. When I got off the plane, she said I was all hunched over like a senior citizen with osteoporosis and seemingly much older than my 39 years.

My first year living with her was mainly spent crying and trying to stand up straight.

Looking back, I realize now how fortunate I was to have had a safe place to go to work through my process. Advice to anyone finding themselves in a similar situation is to look for a place to heal that is as neutral and drama free as possible, a place where love and kindness reside.

It also helps if you are surrounded by the beauty of nature. For me the state of Georgia's sights and sounds of crickets, bull frogs, lightening bugs, colorful cardinals and blue jays, as well as the tall slender pine trees swaying in the warm southern wind, were all a healing balm for my frayed nerves.

Dannie Duncan

***

" No matter what age we are , we can always let go of some more garbage and break a new barrier." (2)

-Louise L. Hay

The hidden wisdom – fasting is good for the soul as well as the body!

<>*<>*<>*<>

<>*<<<*

II MENTAL HEALING

When you are emotionally abused, it affects your mental life. When your mental life is traumatized, your clarity of mind, memory, and intuition are all weakened. Self-worth, as well as your worth to others, gets jaded. Soon, feelings of inadequacy surface, and your emotional intelligence suffers. You start attracting the wrong people into your life. They push your buttons, bruise your ego, or break your heart.

Relationships become strained, and you question if they're even worth it. Your special gifts are hidden from view, and you become closed off. Life in general seems flat, lacking in vibrancy and finesse. Finally, your inner sun becomes so completely over-shadowed by storm clouds that the people you once loved or want to love avoid you like the plague.

It's been said that "in order to let something go you have to first pick it up and recognize it for what it is." So, what exactly is emotional abuse, and how can it be dealt with?

Greg Enns and Jan Black, the authors of the book called, *It's Not Ok Anymore-Your Personal Guide to Ending Abuse, Taking Charge, and Loving Yourself* [1] define emotional abuse as follows:

1. "Taunting you in the name of "fun"."

2. "Ignoring you and/ or your feelings."

3. "Insulting you repeatedly."

4. "Yelling at you."

5. "Telling you, you will fail."

6. "Blaming you for his faults." *(or hers)

7. "Threatening you with violence or retaliation."

8. "Threatening to hurt your pets."

9. "Threatening to abuse the children and/or get custody of them."

10. "Telling you, you must stay because you can't make it alone."

11. "Accusing you of being violent when you protect yourself in any way."

12. "Labeling you as crazy, stupid, bitch, ugly, or a whore." *(cunt, asshole, bastard, etc.)

13. "Blaming you for things that go wrong." *(or trying to steal your joy when things go right)

14. "Holding back approval as a form of punishment." *(or holding back affection such as hugs and kisses, especially in a parent/child relationship)

"Everyone is different, you may also fill in the blanks for yourself."

How to Deal with Emotional Abuse by Utilizing the

Laws for Mental Life

Knowing what emotional abuse looks like is an important first step in getting out from under its oppressive energy and healing from it. Once you identify emotionally abusive behavior in your life, changing your circumstances requires putting healthy boundaries in place.

Do not get a healthy boundary confused with a block. A block is

*Notes from the author Dannie Duncan.

when you close something off completely, whereas a healthy boundary is staying open to something within reasonable limits. If possible, it is always healthier to stay somewhat open and receptive than to close down completely.

OK, so how do you put healthy boundaries in place? Like any challenge it helps if you are equipped with the correct tools for the job.

The tools you need to live life successfully were in place before you even existed. They are called Universal Laws. Most people have heard of laws such as the law of gravity, the law of cause and effect, or the law of thermodynamics, etc.. However, there are literally thousands of laws and principles in existence today that you may have never heard of. They will aid and assist you in your everyday life and positively navigate you to a higher quality of existence.

The universal laws and principles that follow as defined by June G. Bletzer, the author of *The Encyclopedic Psychic Dictionary*, are some that definitely helped me to recover from a nervous breakdown, and they will help you as well in your personal journey toward mental healing.

1. The law of attitude states that: "... 1. –"Attitude" the only weapon that can harm an individual. Nothing, absolutely nothing, in the universe can harm an earthling except his or her own attitude. No human accident, no loss of a loved one, no natural catastrophe, no personal illness, no loss of property, or job hardship can harm one. It is only the attitude one takes toward these events and experiences that hurts the individual. Traumatic experiences are meant to happen in each incarnation. Each experience should be put in the proper perspective, resolved in a favorable manner, analyzed for the good it brought, and balanced with emotionally. Attitude has its degree of emotion and emotion triggers off one's "ongoing-life-process" or one's "ongoing-death-process" in the body. One chooses by his or her attitude which process is to prevail. 2. To whatever depths one sinks below his or her norm, materially, one can rise equally above one's norm, spiritually. One reaches a state wherein nothing material offers any hope and then the soul-mind becomes ready to receive the influx of power and inspiration from the etheric world or the superconscious mind." [2]

An example of applying the law of attitude:

Your boyfriend and you live together and share the bills. He takes money that was meant for the bills and leaves. A whole day and night go by, he doesn't call and there is no trace of him. He has done this before, and your blood boils with anger. You're mad at yourself for putting up with such treatment and embarrassed at the same time.

Instead of making yourself sick, you take a deep breath and try to calm your nerves. You decide to visit your twin sister. Your sister and you decide to go to the movies. You have fun and laugh away the early part of the afternoon. You feel much better and thank your twin for a fun time.

When you get home you call your landlord and the electric company. You make arrangements to pay your bills on another day. To your relief, the roof over your head and the electric service are secured.

You check your mailbox, and there is an unexpected check in it. You cash it and buy a few groceries. Later that night your boyfriend comes home and explains that he left because he had stress on his job and felt he needed to get away to think. You take his story with a grain of salt but are relieved that he is back. He apologizes and decides to work an extra shift the next day to make up for the money he took.

When you change your attitude to positive, things around you change to positive because like energy, attracts like energy.

Note: *It helps to picture your mind as a nice home and your thoughts as people that knock at your home's door. Do not let people in (thoughts, words, or deeds) that are dirty, nasty, or negative. If they sneak in thru a* *window, sic the dog on them. Or if you have to let them in, make them take a shower or at the very least, take off their shoes! Guard your mind from negative thinking as you guard your home from negative intruders. Give a warm welcome to your positive visitors (thoughts). In following this Law of Attitude, those who would - seek to, or unknowingly - hurt you with their negativity will be stopped in their tracks.*

2. **The Law of Holding on** states that: "... Any activity one starts, whether it be a poem, a craft, a home, a love, a job, etc. should be worked at until it is finished as perfectly as one can make it. The joy is in the moments of the making, not the finished product. This law goes further to say that one should hold onto an object or human relationship *only* as long as it makes a learning experience for one. [**cf**. Law of Letting Go]." [2]

<u>**An example of applying the law of holding on**</u>:

Your girlfriend slowly becomes more and more controlling. Nothing you say or do is good enough for her anymore.

You notice she spends more and more time on the computer. When you approach her while she is on it, she gets annoyed and minimizes the screen.

She starts criticizing your hair, your weight, and how you dress. She taunts and makes fun of you. It feels as if you are walking on egg shells all the time, and you cannot do anything right.

Finally, she asks you to become her roommate instead of her live-in boyfriend and wants to start seeing other people. You ask her to go to counseling with you, but she refuses. You're devastated but consider saying yes to the arrangement she's suggesting because you love her so much.

However, after some soul searching, you decide to move out and start dating other people. You are sad but know instinctively that you are doing the best thing for yourself and for her. You know you deserve to be

Dannie Duncan

Some universal laws and principles are emotional, some are mental, some are physical, and some are spiritual by nature. Whether you know it or not, these laws and principles govern everything you and others do.

The hidden wisdom – *when you learn how to utilize universal laws and principles, you'll have an advantage and your life will improve!*

with someone who *wants* to be with you, someone who will love you back.

A month after moving out, you meet someone new. Eventually, you marry this person and live happily into your future.

Note: *If what you are doing, and who you are doing it with, is causing you harm or blocking your purpose on any level, finish that and move on. We are here to learn and to enjoy the ride, and these are keys!*

3. **The Law of Letting Go** states that: "…One should say good-bye without regrets or resentment to anything or anyone that is no longer useful and purposeful in making or adding to a learning experience for one's self (whether it be a home, record, plant, animal, former love, car, a grown child, club membership, philosophy, belief, lifestyle, book, etc.). The pleasure should be in the moment of the doing, the making, or the learning, with the object or experience. This frees one to begin another learning experience without bondage to the old image of one's self. (Don Juan) "One should erase personal history by dropping past friends, relatives, cities, and events; where one has been and what one has done, so no one builds a fog around you or is angry with you." [**cf**. New-Age Psychology]" [2]

An example of applying the law of letting go:

You are a hair stylist and take the first job you find right out of cosmetology school. There is not much education at the salon, and you learn everything the hard way. Slowly but surely, you master your skills and build up a clientele of which to be proud.

The salon owner is unprofessional and makes unreasonable demands on you and all the other stylists. Eventually, everyone quits but you. A few months go by and the only customers in the salon are yours. The owner comes in with her boyfriend and just sits and watches you cut hair, then, she criticizes your techniques. You feel stifled and depressed with your current situation. You decide to look for a happier and more professional salon to work. Your search is rewarded, and you find the perfect fit. You tell your new employers that you need to give your current employer a generous notice, and they agree.

You call a meeting with your current boss. You thank her for everything she has taught you, and then you explain that you have found another position elsewhere that is a better fit for you. You tell her that hers is the first and only salon you have ever worked and you feel it is time to further your horizons. You give her a generous notice and there are no hard feelings. She says you are welcome to come back to her salon at any time and that she will visit you at your new place of employment.

Note: *In order for new, healthy people or situations to come in, old, unhealthy relationships or situations need to be cleared out, and you will then be free to reinvent yourself.*

4.   **The Law of Opposites** states that: "... Everything has a reverse relationship. Anything can be split into two complete reverse characteristics, and each of these reverse characteristics contains the essence of the other in its essence. Each end of polarity contains the potentiality of the elements of the other. One pole away from a central fixation has its reverse characteristic the same distance or density from the center; eg., positive/negative, hot/cold, loud/quiet, yin/yang, lingam/yoni, male/female, sick/well, happy/sad, up/down, black/white, stale/fresh. The Slavs have two deities in the etheric world , Byelbog and Chernobog; personifying Darkness and Light, Good and Evil, used together as if both were a part of the one; similar to Christianity's God and Satan. [**cf.** Law of Polarity.]"[2]

An example of applying the law of opposites:

You decide to take up the hobby of archery. As you strive to hit your target, you either over-shoot or under-shoot your arrow. This goes on for several weeks. Then as you continue to practice, you eventually balance your skills and to your delight when you release your next shot, the arrow hits the center of the bull's-eye.

Note: *You live in a world of duality. In this realm you could not experience the positive without the negative with which to compare it. This is the fullness of life. There is a Buddhist teaching which states "...one's enemy is the best teacher."* [3] *As you look back over your life, you must admit that your greatest lessons have often come from the most miserable people.*

5. The Principle of Wellness states that: "...Wellness – a degree of mental and physical health that one feels comfortable with and tries to maintain; the responsibility for good health and future health rests with one's self; 1. what is good health for one is not necessarily good health for another; a State of Consciousness wherein one can relate to one's self and feel satisfied with one's behavior and lifestyle; good health is not a measurement of one's spiritual growth; how one handles one's wealth is not a method for preventing illness; 2. to balance, resolve, and put in proper perspective the stresses of everyday experiences, without postponing these stresses for future handling, contributes to good health; 3. emphasis should be on a lifestyle that brings harmonious integration of the Soul-Mind and the Conscious Mind to bring correct health for the body in this incarnation. [**cf.** New-Age Psychology, Curative Education, Holism]" [2]

An example of applying the principle of wellness:

You are under a great deal of stress at work and in your personal life. You try not to think about it or talk about it. As a result, you keep your problems bottled up inside. You make time for everyone else but yourself.

Then instead of eating right, taking vitamins, exercising, meditating, and getting enough rest, you ignore these things and your health. You work 24/7 and run your life on empty. You scramble like a rabbit right up until the last day before your long-awaited vacation.

On day one of your vacation, you come down with the flu, and it lasts right up until the day before you are to return to work.

Note: *The best antidote for what ails you is two doses of its opposite three times a day.*

Signs that you are healing mentally is a thirst for authenticity and an overwhelming desire to be happy and to see others happy.

Possible Pitfalls on the Road to Mental Healing:

When life gets tough you may feel like you are the only one who has ever suffered thus. However, the truth is that there is nothing you are experiencing that another has not suffered before you. If you are lucky enough to find the clues they've left behind on how they dealt with their problems through word of mouth, on-line sources, or in books etc., it will greatly assist you in avoiding these same traps and pitfalls.

If you will but follow the breadcrumbs great teachers left behind, it will be to your benefit. And, you *will* find and follow the right path, simply by consciously seeking it.

Joshua David Stone, the author of, *Soul Psychology: How To Clear Negative Emotions And Spiritualize Your Life* [4] left breadcrumbs for us in the form of his definitions of Pitfalls and Traps on the path of ascension. In his book Stone recommends avoiding the following temptations in order to facilitate a better life:

1. "Thinking the earth is a terrible place."

    The earth is what you think it is; thoughts become things.

2. "Being the Savior."

They say that if your plane is going down to take oxygen yourself first before trying to save others. Metaphorically speaking, do you always give your oxygen away to others first to the point of risking brain damage to yourself?

3. "Allowing yourself to go on autopilot and losing your vigilance."

It is important to live consciously and not sleepwalk through your life. Make worthy goals, and do not give up until they become a reality, period.

4. "The trap of glamour of power, and holding power over others once you become successful."

Be *humbly grateful.*

You Can Say "Yes" or You Can Say "No" To Define Healthy Mental Boundaries!

If you have suffered through long-term emotional abuse, chances are you were never taught by example or told how to put healthy boundaries in place. A healthy boundary is simply a personal guideline you adhere to for your own optimal health.

If you were fortunate enough to have had adults in your life that modeled healthy boundaries as well as put them in place for you when you were too young to do it for yourself, you are one of the lucky ones. Sadly, this is often not the case, and you may have been unprepared when abuse presented itself. When you become aware of the concept of healthy boundaries, it is never too late to start implementing them for yourself.

Draw a metaphorical line in the sand that says "cross this line and I will make changes in our relationship." You choose the behaviors you'll accept for your own health and well-being and communicate that to others. You draw the lines in the sand, and you define your personal boundaries because you are worthy of respect. Remember that you must put healthy emotional, spiritual, mental, and physical boundaries in place, or at some point, you may be taken advantage of on any one of those levels.

The thing to remember if you are ever compromised is that you have the personal choice of seeing the person mistreating you as either an abuser or an abuse victim. If you choose to see him/her as an abuse victim, ill, or in need of help - which is often the case with an abuser - you will then be free to stand in a position of power. In a power position, you may practice compassion which can be a healing force for everyone involved. This may be easier said than done if there is evil intent involved, but a worthy goal never the less!

If you are temporarily unable to put physical boundaries in place because of circumstances beyond your immediate control, you can still put up emotional, mental, and/or spiritual boundaries. This is how many of the survivors of the Holocaust held on during WWII. Many prisoners while enduring unspeakable atrocities, managed to stay sane by keeping their minds engaged in thoughts of future goals or reuniting with their loved ones.

And if they could do it, you can, too!

The ones that survived kept strong, positive thought-boundaries in place as hidden treasure and those thought-boundaries kept their life-blood pumping until they either escaped or were rescued. It is inspiring to read some of the holocaust survivors' stories – if you ever get the chance - their examples will live on forever, and are a gift to all of us.

"...when I say "no" to you, I am saying" yes" to me." (5)

–Louise L. Hay

Say "Yes," or Say "No" to Define Your Mental Boundaries

*Say "yes" to self-definition and say "no" to ever letting another person label you in any way.

*Say "yes" to temporary guilt and say "no" to permanent shame. Guilt is when you feel bad about something you've done and attempt to make amends for that, and then forgive yourself and let it go. Shame is when you feel bad about self, and shame will stay with you for a lifetime if you let it. The truth is that you are always perfect the way God made you.

*Say "yes" to positive thoughts words and deeds, and say "no" to negatives on any front.

*Say "yes" to see all as sacred and enjoying the journey, and say "no" to the pain and torment of attachment or aversion; clinging or repelling triggers negative emotions which can lead to heartache.

Great Teachers Have Expressed Words,

Which Will Make A Difference In Your Mental Healing:

Once in a while in life you run across teachers who say something in just the right way and at just the right time to change who you are forever. At that moment in time, they become your healers. Read the following statements from some great teachers and let these statements mentally soothe you:

"...change the way you look at things, and the things you look at will change." [6] "My feeling bad will only ensure that I attract more of feeling bad into my life." [7]

—Wayne Dyer

"Of course, worry, fear, and all negative thoughts produce a crop after their kind; those who harbor thoughts of this kind must inevitably reap what they have sown." [8]

—Charles F. Haanel

Dannie Duncan

"These thoughts, words, and actions produce feelings; and our feelings become the currency with which we purchase our life experiences." [9]

—Louise L. Hay and Cheryl Richardson

"Once you are on the road, fully committed to being responsible for yourself and stopping the blame, success is almost certain." [10]

—Lucinda Bassett

"What you think of me is none of my business." [11]

—Terry Cole-Whittaker

"Belief in oneself is required for healing." [12]

—Caroline Myss, PH.D.

Recommended Reading That Will Help You

On Your Journey Toward Mental Healing:

1. *The Secret,* by Rhonda Byrne

2. *The Power,* by Rhonda Byrne

3. *The Magic,* by Rhonda Byrne

4. *The Essential ZOHAR: The Source of Kabbalistic Wisdom,* by Rav P.S. Berg

5. *Ask and It Is Given: Learning to Manifest Your Desires,* by Esther and Jerry Hicks

6. *Why People Don't Heal and How They Can,* by Caroline Myss,

P.H. D

7. *The Ascended Masters Light the Way, Beacons Of Ascension,*

by Joshua David Stone, Ph.D.

8 . *The Kyballion, A study of the Hermetic Philosophy of Ancient*

Egypt and Greece, by The Three Initiates

9. *Gratitude: A Way of Life,* by Louise L. Hay and Friends

Dannie Duncan

If someone has been in the dark for a long time and asks you for a light, don't hand them a chandelier; you'll blind them.

The hidden wisdom - *don't force your opinions on others or allow others to force their opinions on you, you'll both get hurt!*

✱ₓ**✱**ₓ**✱**

The therapist informed me that I was like an anorexic in that an anorexic doesn't recognize hunger and has to be told when to eat. I didn't recognize disrespect and had to be clued in to when it was going on in a form too subtle for me to recognize or too bold for me to believe it was what it was.

The hidden wisdom - *you will <u>not</u> get from others what you <u>will not</u> give to yourself!*

III BREAKDOWN

Part I: Breakdown - Sex Addicts

My Life With a Sex Addict Named Ayden

If you find yourself involved with a sex addict look within yourself first to discover what it was about you that drew them to you in the first place. Remember –"like energy attracts like energy."

I moved out of my parents' home and in with an older African-American man named Ayden when I was 18 years old. His skin was the color of rich dark chocolate, and he smelled of incense and cherries. He was upbeat, fun-loving, and really enjoyed music. Ayden was always dancing around the room, and trying to get me to dance with him.

When we were together Ayden gave me his undivided attention and I often felt like the center of his universe. I'd never experienced a man like him before, and for a young inexperienced girl with low self-esteem he was intoxicating. To me he symbolized an introduction to an exotic new world.

In Ayden, I was also trying to satisfy my long-held curiosity about the black race. I was after all of mixed parents, yet raised in a Caucasian household. At the same time, I was subconsciously seeking a father figure to love and accept me.

A part of me knew that he wasn't the right partner for me, but another part hoped that he would be the one who would help me to feel whole, chase away my fears.

When I met Ayden, he was legally separated from his wife and planning on getting a divorce. The fact that he was married should have been a deal breaker for me, however growing up I had - on occasion - witnessed my stepfather and mother pursuing extra marital affairs. Looking back, I believe I formed a subconscious idea that this type of behavior was just a natural part of adult life.

His mother was only fourteen years old when she had Ayden. He was raised by his grandfather and taken out of school at a young age to work on his grandpa's farm in Arkansas. When I met him he could only read at a fourth grade level. Because of his lack of education it was hard for him to find a decent job. He worked as a janitor cleaning medical buildings at night and detailed cars on the side during the day. He took private classes to learn how to read. I admired him for that. His dream was to own his own restaurant.

Even though Ayden was 12 years older than me, he was immature and lacked self-discipline. He encouraged me to open credit card accounts and used the accounts to start several small businesses that ultimately ended in failure. In my youth, I was blind to the havoc these mounting credit card bills would play on my future credit rating when the payments got out of hand.

I soon realized that Ayden was a player with a sex addiction, but by that time, I was in too deep to just leave. I had invested my heart and given my virginity to him as well. As time went on, he was seeing others girls on the side. When I suspected that he was cheating and spoke up, he'd always say that the other women were just friends or business partners. I wanted to believe him, and so I did.

Over time, our relationship transformed into me being more of a parent and he being more of a child.

At that point, I began turning off sexually. Ayden responded by forcing painful sex on me. This went on for days at a time. It was draining. I'd lay there and pray to be released from the monotony of what was becoming a sick ritual. One night as he was forcing himself on me, I got up in the middle of what seemed an episode that would never end, and I told him that I was going to sleep on top of the hope chest at the foot of our bed. It was hard and cold, but I just lay down on it like it was my new mattress. He got scared that I was losing my mind and the forced sex ended.

As time passed by we argued more and more. These scenes always ended with me crying hysterically and with him calmly insisting that nobody would ever love me the way that he did. We were both miserable, and our life together was exhausting. I was an emotional wreck, and he was confused and would often feel drained by me.

I wanted to leave Ayden with every fiber of my being, but he was very possessive. I was scared and didn't know quite how to go about it.

It finally turned out that I didn't have to. One night, our relationship came to a screeching halt. Ayden came home and asked me to move out because he was in love with someone else. She was pregnant. That was that. I acted sad, yet it felt as if a great weight had been lifted off of my shoulders. It was as if I had suddenly woken up from a bad dream. I moved out hoping it would be the clean break I'd been waiting for, but it didn't turn out that way. Ayden went on to stalk me and my parents for the next seven years.

My take on Sex Addicts

What is a sex addict? Sex addicts are people whom use sex like a drug. They can never get enough. And, no matter how hard you try to satisfy them you cannot, because it's not about you, it's about the conquest.

They will often brag, "Don't hate the player; hate the game!"

..*

"While on a blind date with a gun packing biker that I had met on a chat-line, I found myself alone with him in a secluded wooded area at night. He asked me to get out of his truck, walked me to the middle of a bridge over-looking a black body of water, and then just stood there saying nothing. I thought I was dead.

As I peered downward into the black murky water, I thought to myself, "I don't want to die like this; nobody will even be able to find my body!" Thoughts of my mother wondering where I was, and my son growing up without a mother raced through my mind. I'd reached my limit.

I broke the silence and asked my blind date if he was going to kill me. He simply said, "If I'm going to kill you – it's too late now – so you might as well stop worrying about it, right?" I couldn't argue with that so I stopped worrying. I would live to see another day.

He took me back to his trailer, then expressed that I wasn't really his type; he liked spiky- haired redheads, with tattoos and body piercings. That was definitely not me. My hair was brown and shoulder length. My skin was a virgin canvas, and the only things pierced were my ears.

It was ludicrous but somehow I felt inadequate.

For the next twenty minutes he showed me all of his knives and guns hidden on his person and around his trailer.

He pointed to a picture of his wife on the wall. I didn't know he had a wife! She was gorgeous and looked like Stevie Nicks from Fleetwood Mac in her younger days. I was wondering why he would cheat on such a beautiful woman. He said she worked nights and was at work right then. At that moment she called. He instructed me to be quiet. I got paranoid, like maybe they were in on this together.

After he hung up the phone he showed me some of her artwork and talked a little about him and her. I got the impression that he loved her more than she loved him. I felt empathy for a moment.

Then he showed me a picture of himself in his younger days. In the picture he had long blonde hair down to his waist and he was posing in front of a Harley Davidson motorcycle on Hollywood Blvd, in Los Angeles California. He was dressed in black leather from head to toe.

In spite of my fear I had to admit that he was hot.

He revealed to me that he considered himself a Satanist. I'm thinking, "Great, what else can go wrong!" He asked me to undress and after fearing for my life and then witnessing all of his knives and guns, I wasn't about to say no at that point.

He put on a rubber which surprised me. We had sex and when it was over he told me that I'd been video-taped.

He said if I ever became famous he would sell the pictures for money. I was mortified. There went my shot at politics or ever hoping to be on Oprah!

When it was over, he drove me back to my car and kissed me goodbye. The kiss seemed out of context to the evening as a whole, and was strangely out of character.

He advised me to never do anything like this again because it was dangerous. "No shit", I thought to myself!

That experience woke me up, and taught me more in a single night than I'd learned in two whole years of therapy.

After the trauma of that blind date, I got off of Zoloft (which I had been taking for two years for anxiety), I stopped dating, and I quit therapy. I learned my lesson and would never knowingly put myself in a dangerous position like that ever again. I would finally be safe with myself.

Over the next two years that followed, it became clear to me about who I was and what I wanted in relationship. However, as a result of that night I developed a reaction formation. A reaction formation is defined as "… a behavioral tendency developed in direct opposition to a repressed impulse."[1]

I cut my hair into a really short spike and dyed it a bold bright red. For the next eight years nobody could talk me into wearing my hair in any other way.

The hidden wisdom *– a person is healthy when he or she is safe with him or herself; this includes keeping oneself out of harm's way.*

Living your life with any kind of addict may seem exhilarating in the beginning because they can be fun-loving, charismatic, and a *rush* to be with, but that soon fizzles out and then living or dealing with them can become particularly *grueling.*

When you first meet a sex addict, you're taken aback by their passionate persistence. They'll call you every night. You may go dancing together, to the movies, or out to dinner a few times a week. They'll send flowers to your job, give a gift to your child, or buy you a new outfit that actually fits. Before you even divulge your home address, you may find they've left you intimate items in your mailbox such as sexy underwear or a vibrator. This move has a mild stalker vibe that is disturbing yet at the same time is an adrenaline-rush. Be careful here because it is easy to get addicted to that *adrenaline rush,* and they move in fast at this point and try to get you into the *sack.*

In the beginning you'll find you have a lot to talk about with the sex addict, and you'll feel like the center of their universe. They can be so emotionally supportive that you'll swear that they are both male and female in one body, everything you need. They love to laugh and have fun. They'll try to keep you stoned or liquored up. If they at all suspect you're falling for them, they may divulge a strict set of double standard rules for you to follow. It goes downhill from there.

How Do You know if You're in a Relationship With a Sex Addict?

Sex addicts get frequent text messages, cell phone calls, and emails that they never share with you. In a live-in situation calls may come into the home phone where the caller hangs up when *you* say hello. When you casually mention this to your partner, he/she accuses you of getting the calls and having an affair.

It's because they're cheating and they are projecting their infidelity on to you. Addicts often do that.

They may spend hours on the computer. If you walk up on them while their on it they'll try to distract you from looking at the screen by minimizing it, switching the screen or blocking your view with their body. They may stand up and face you, or seem agitated and fidgety until you leave.

"Opposite sex" friendships are routine with sex addicts. They will tell you that this is how it has always been for them. They just get along better with the opposite sex. Or, they may tell you that all these acquaintances are potential business partners. These business partners give them money, but they are seldom or never friendly with you.

Whether you are gay or straight, if you find yourself consistently jealous for no apparent reason – and you cannot shake the feeling – trust your instincts. You are jealous because you feel their energy disconnecting from yours, and you are not imagining it.

Weekends roll around and you think you and your partner will spend time together, instead, they say they're going to run a quick errand, and you won't see them again for several hours. This happens time and time again.

If it's a guy, he'll tell you that he went to look at cars or to the golf range to shoot some balls or he ran into a buddy. If it's a woman, she'll say she went shopping or visiting with her mother or a friend. She may say she went to look at model homes or to the library. The destinations may be different, but the reasons are the same. They are with their lovers.

Don't be surprised if someone knocks at your front door and then cries or gets mad when they see you before storming off. He/she truly thought they were in a relationship with your partner, and seeing you at his or her place of residence shocks them. When you confront your mate about it, your partner will say that it's not his/her fault. This person was just a friend or a business partner who became enamored with him/her, and then after that they couldn't shake them.

Count your money often because they may take small amounts from your purse or wallet when you're not looking. You'll notice that they will treat you lavishly with *your* money.

I know this is ugly, but hang in here with me...

When you go for a drive with a sex addict, they will be nervously watching the cars around you to make sure they're not being followed.

They may try to teach you how *not* to be followed, secretly afraid of being caught in their infidelity, or worse yet being attacked by an angry lover's spouse.

A sex addict may want you to get checked for an infection or venereal disease, because then - when you find out they have one - they can accuse you of giving it to them.

They will instigate a fight so they have an excuse to leave the house, then they will go out partying without you. This may happen more often around the holidays when you are distracted by all the hustle bustle of shopping and entertaining.

Your family members and friends are not safe from their overtures either. The sex addict may flirt with them shamelessly. You could find out that they've slept with your own sister or brother - or even worse - your mother or father!

Lastly you'll get unexpected gifts. Sex addicts will buy you gifts whenever they start a new fling or feel guilty when they have carried a fling too far.

Caution: When you finally leave a sex-addicted relationship, get counseling. You may walk away from this relationship taking addictive behavior patterns with you without even realizing it. These addictive behavior patterns can manifest in the form of procrastination, over-eating, depression, anxiety, or living on the edge by taking unnecessary chances.

These patterns may result in bouncing checks, getting write-ups at work, not paying your bills on time, getting poor credit scores, receiving traffic tickets, gaining weight, going on risky blind dates, shopping uncontrollably, sleeping too much or not enough etc... ; the list goes on, and it's not pretty.

Dannie Duncan

It was the very first therapy session I had ever attended. After brief introductions the first thing the psychologist said to me was, "You will be OK, I promise." And, she was right!

The hidden wisdom – *"A journey of a thousand miles begins with a single step."*

-Loa-tzu, The Way of Lao-tzu

Chinese philosopher (604 BC – 531BC)

Part II. Breakdown - Gamblers

My Life With a Gambler Named Nate!

I*f you go in to relationship thinking you can change the other person, you will be disappointed. Remember, you can only change yourself.*

Rather than taking the time to grow up and heal after my relationship with Ayden, I moved to Las Vegas Nevada to begin a new relationship with Nate who was sixteen years my senior.

Nate stood a little over six feet tall. He was a mix of Mohawk Indian, French, and African-American. His skin was light, and his eyes were sky blue. The hair on his head was thick and chock-full of golden brown curls. Nate played jazz guitar and wrote music and poetry. I was smitten.

However, partnering with him was like jumping from the frying pan into the fire.

When Nate and I first met, he informed me that he was legally separated from his wife and planning to get a divorce. I believed him. He had joint custody of their three children.

Again, I should have walked away right then and not dated him until his divorce was final, but I didn't. Instead, I moved full steam ahead with our relationship and eventually moved in with him, requiring little for myself and knowing relatively little about him.

Nate was unemployed when I first met him; however he said that he had just sold a song he had written to the country singer, Waylon Jennings. His ultimate dream was to direct movies and write screen plays. He had lofty goals for himself and explained to me that he would either make it big or not, but he would never work at a menial job. This was because he was raised by a father who was a workaholic, whom he rarely got to spend time with. He promised himself that he would not turn out the same way. At first I saw him as a starving artist type and it held a certain charm for me.

The charm soon faded.

It took a while for me to discover that he had a gambling problem as well as a sleeping disorder that made him sleepwalk in the middle of the night and eat large amounts of food from the kitchen. He seldom worked, but for some reason, even though I worked two jobs, we were always broke and hungry.

Selling our blood for money became a way to make a few extra dollars. We had no vehicle, had to walk everywhere and had little to eat. I would often feel nauseous and dizzy after selling blood, and would want to go home to lie down. However, instead of going home, Nate would insist that we stroll through various casinos and look for money left behind in slot machine trays. If we were lucky, we'd scrounge enough money to buy two slices of pizza.

Still, Nate always seemed as if he wanted the best for us, and together we would come up with plans to better our situation.

We decided to move from Las Vegas to Los Angeles, California. I was planning on attending trade school. Nate had a friend who owned a furniture reupholstering business, and his friend offered him an in-house position. I got a job in an eye clinic and started school to become an optician.

We found a small one bedroom apartment and were hopeful that this would be the fresh start that we both needed.

At that point Nate's wife sent all three of their children to move in with us in our one bedroom apartment. Our place was too small for all of us, we had no car, and we were barely making ends meet.

In hindsight, good for her; it was a great plan of revenge against the "other woman."

Nate eventually quit his sales job to stay home every day with the kids while I was working and going to school. Both of our stress levels increased tremendously, but he began to complain a lot. The added responsibility pushed us both to our limits, and more stress was on the way.

I became pregnant. My thyroid started giving me problems and the doctors put me on bed rest for the first three months; I had to quit work and school, giving up my short-term goal to become an optician.

Even though things were really rough at that point, I wanted Nate to divorce his wife and marry me so that our baby would be born in a state of wedlock. He said that he couldn't marry me because he didn't have the money to pursue getting a divorce. In my delicate state of health - with a high-risk pregnancy – I was too fatigued to argue. However, the whole situation caused mounting anxiety.

Nate decided that he didn't like the weight I was gaining during my pregnancy, so he started to monitor everything I ate. He was overweight himself but insisted that he couldn't be with a woman who was heavy, pregnant or not.

He would instigate arguments, and the tension between us would cause my nose to bleed. When he'd see the blood running down my face and top, it would scare him and the arguing would stop.

It was mid-December and Christmas was right around the corner. Christmas morning rolled around, and we had no money to put any presents under the tree for his kids.

Even though my parents struggled financially, they had always managed to make Christmas special for me when I was growing up. The looks on the children's faces when they woke up and saw the vacant space under the Christmas tree, broke my heart.

Pregnant or not, two adults collecting unemployment benefits while trying to care for three children just wasn't cutting it. Nate got a lead on a driver position for a traveling band. When he asked me my opinion about his accepting the position I said, "No way." That would have left me pregnant and alone to fend for myself with three kids in a one bedroom apartment with no money, no friends or relatives, and no transportation in a bad part of town. His kids weren't getting along at that point and I was having trouble controlling them. I had around-the-clock morning sickness and just wasn't up for the challenge of handling things by myself while Nate traveled for extended periods of time with a road band.

With my decision Nate got discouraged and stopped looking for work all together. His reaction caused me to second guess myself; however I knew at that point that he had given up completely on trying to find work. I was the one who was going to have to look for a job.

The morning sickness disappeared in my seventh month of pregnancy, so I got a job right away. I found a position at an information desk in a shopping mall. That job lasted a couple of months, and then I went on to work in a sheepskin store at the same mall.

We didn't have a car, so I took three city buses to get to and from work, and many times I'd fall asleep on the buses between stops from sheer exhaustion. When I'd awaken, people would be staring at me; no doubt, I'd been snoring. I caught the bus home from work around 9:P.M., and if I wasn't alert, the bus driver wouldn't see me waiting there in the dark of night and would whiz on by, resulting in me having to wait another hour for the next bus.

By 10:00 p. m. in Los Angeles, California, homeless people would come to rest on the bench beside me, unhappy that I was in their regular spot.

As time went on and I established myself in my new job, things were finally beginning to balance out at home with Nate and the kids. We were in sync and starting to feel like a real family. At that point Nate's wife abruptly pulled the kids out of our home and back to live with her. We were all caught off guard and saddened with the sudden change. I couldn't help but think that she timed it that way to disrupt our sense of well-being.

Enter Baby!

As a 31-year-old woman whose biological clock had been ticking for quite a while, I still felt that the pregnancy was a God-send in spite of my less than fortunate circumstances.

However when my water broke, I went into labor in the middle of working in a shopping mall. My boss paid an Australian cabby to rush me to the hospital through noon-day Los Angeles traffic.

My son Bret was born by cesarean section after two days of hard labor. He was born with the cord wrapped around his neck, and he wasn't breathing. Everyone in the birthing room held their breath until they heard Bret gasp for air. When we realized he was going to be ok, there was communal sigh of relief. They brought him to my bedside. He was beautiful; he had fair skin, golden hair, and his dad's sky blue eyes. I loved my new baby boy very much, but I had no idea how hard the next five years would be for him and me.

Desperate Times!

After our son was born, Nate - the baby's father - started hanging around people that were doing things that were illegal, things like stealing luggage from airports and selling the goods, or renting furniture, then selling it and telling the rental company that it had been stolen. They tried to talk him into joining them. I would protest and seemingly talked Nate out of every devious invitation.

Since the in-house upholstery position didn't work out for Nate, he got a job at a designer fashion warehouse shortly following our son's birth so I could stay home with our baby. After working only one week, he brought me home some designer clothes from his job; they were all wet and muddy from being dropped in the rainstorm. It was the only gift he had ever given me.

The next day he got a call from his boss threatening him with arrest if he didn't bring the clothes back immediately. He told me that they had given them to him, but they said that he had taken them without their permission. He got fired the next day.

I seriously questioned Nate's character at that point, but I felt deeply weary by the post-partum fatigue and depression that were slowly over-taking me.

When no other job opportunities panned out for Nate in Los Angeles, we eventually moved back to Las Vegas. Things swiftly went from bad to worse. Nate started yelling constantly, and I began wearing earplugs to avoid getting headaches from the sheer volume of his voice. I was miserable and stressed much of the time. More pressures were added when Nate's wife unexpectedly drove in from Los Angeles to Las Vegas to drop off their two sons to live with us again; she kept her daughter with her that time. The boys seemed as surprised as we were at their arrival.

I found work, and we tried to hold things together.

As time went on Nate would use my or the kids social security numbers for various scams without permission. He insisted that nothing be put in his own name.

Eventually, I had no money or credit left to my name and a mountain of debt.

Although, I was far from perfect, everything Nate stood for went against all of my internal instincts.

As the situation worsened, I began to breakdown both emotionally and physically. I sensed that something was wrong with me; I told Nate that I needed professional counseling. He disagreed and said that he could counsel me. He told me that he had taken several psychology classes in the past and that he could be my therapist. We had that same conversation about three times. Nothing ever came from it. In hindsight, I believe I was reaching out for his help feeling unable to help myself. We both ignored my warning signs.

As my depression grew worse, I reached out to a male co-worker. We soon began an emotional affair. Sensing I was vulnerable, he pursued a relationship with me.

At home Nate seemed unhappy and we were swiftly growing apart. He finally found a job at a local warehouse. It was the first job he had found in a long time. I felt a small sense of relief. We needed the money and I was hopeful that the job would cheer him up.

However, my secret emotional affair at work combined with our financial stresses that had built up over-time, eventually dismantled our relationship. Nate finally told me, "I can take you or leave you." With that I allowed my emotional affair with my co-worker to turn into a physical one. When that happened, I immediately told Nate the truth and moved out.

By the time we split up, I felt paranoid, suffocated, exhausted, and overworked.

At that moment, I had no choice but to leave our son Bret where he was ...with his father and two older half brothers (Nate's sons) that had come to live with us.

In hindsight I was acting out of a state of desperation, and I was not thinking logically about what I was about to do.

The decision I made in that state would soon come to haunt me.

Understandably things became very ugly after that. Nate was furious with me. He would call me at work and threaten violence. I was advised to get a restraining order.

One afternoon, I went to Bret's school to pick him up and walk him home to my apartment for our regular visit. I soon discovered that his dad had already gotten him. The school office said that Nate asked that I no longer be allowed to pick him up.

I became hysterical and the schools' female principal had to calm me down.

Nate admitted to me later that he had made that decision because of the restraining order. He thought I was going to try to keep him from his son.

The thought of keeping Nate from his son, never even crossed my mind, and I was in shock that he was seeking revenge in this form. I realized at that moment that I had to work with Nate in whatever way I could to protect our son from being used as a pawn.

The school principal recommended that I back down and allow Bret to live with his dad, remain in the same school and have the same routine for his optimal well-being. Even though her advice had merit, I found out later that this same principal was making flirtatious passes at Nate during the same time frame that she had given me this advice.

I finally called a law firm to find out what my rights were concerning custody. The lawyer on the phone was harsh but straight forward with me. She said because Nate was already married and had other children that lived with him, I stood no chance what-so-ever in a court of law.

When I told her that up until recently I had been the sole breadwinner she said that made things even worse for me. Furthermore, she pointed out that there were strict abandonment limitations in Nevada that I had exceeded.

Even though I was picking Bret up from school every day and walking him home, volunteering at his school, and bringing him home with me for overnight visits...Nate was lying and telling everyone that I had abandoned my son. He was also demanding lump sums of money from me in exchange for being able to see Bret. I had to make appointments with my manager at work to ask for advances on my salary to accommodate his demands.

I began to cry hysterically. She seemed surprised by my outburst and then softened her tone with me. Completely disheartened, I ended our telephone conversation. I cried nonstop for the next three days.

Although we eventually would share custody of our son Bret, he lived primarily with Nate for the next three and a half years. During that time I ached for him every day.

In hindsight, it was the best decision for Bret at that time because despite my depression and emotional instability, I jumped right into another destructive relationship with my "co-worker", Stan.

And, he turned out to be a womanizer.

This man would take me to Oregon, even further from my son and would eventually push me over the edge.

Fast Forward - When the dust finally settled - at the four-year mark, my son Bret came to live with me full-time. By then my coworker Stan and I had split up, and I lived in the state of Georgia with my mother.

During the next decade that followed, I moved out of my mother's house with Bret and got my own place. I underwent extensive psychological treatment and counseling. I pursued a path of self education in the study of spiritual enlightenment and enrichment. I devoured hundreds of self help, motivational and metaphysical books during my journey.

I still made mistakes (mostly inconsequential), but I slowly became emotionally and physically stronger. Gradually I evolved into a strong role model to Bret, and the kind of parent that he deserved.

I went back to college (part-time) to try to fulfill my long-lost dream of getting a degree in psychology.

Bret lived with me until he graduated valedictorian from high school in a class with over a thousand members. He moved northeast that fall to attend an Ivy League college with a full-ride, academic scholarship. He attended school in England during his junior year, and traveled to Spain on his break. He had learned to speak fluent Spanish in high school and then continued studying it in college. He took up the Chinese language as well.

He graduated and was awarded a BA in Neuroscience and Philosophy.

At the time of this writing, he is attending graduate school at a prestigious mid-western college. He is pursuing a dual PhD in education and cognitive science and the study of how people learn.

He's dating a nice Chinese girl in the college's foreign exchange program.

He still bears some emotional baggage from his years in a dysfunctional situation but - in general- is doing quite well.

Note: Nate, my son's father, never did get a divorce from his wife and to this day they continue to live separate lives. He still writes music & poetry and hopes to sell a screenplay someday.

My Take on Gamblers

Who are gamblers? Gamblers are people addicted to living on the edge with their money, or whatever else they have to wager. When you first meet gamblers, you are charmed by the twinkle in their eye and their tall tales of half-truths. You feel like they really understand you, because everything you're into, they're into.

When you live with a gambler, it feels as if you're living with a human vacuum cleaner. No matter what you have in the form of material goods, it gets sucked away never to be seen again.

Gambling is just like any other addiction. You will never make enough money to keep enough food in the fridge, money in the bank, or clothes on your back, because the money is funneled out into his/her addiction. Because of this, keeping a roof over your head will be a constant challenge.

Gamblers may ask you questions like, "What would you do if someone offered you a million dollars to sleep with them?" And, they may ask questions like this once every few months because they're intrigued with the concept.

Gamblers *seem* success oriented and supportive of your dreams and goals. Be careful here and really listen to them. They will give you excuses as to why they haven't realized their own dreams and will always talk as if they are on the precipice of something big.

If you bring anything of value into these relationships, beware. Your things will end up at the pawn shop or lost from storage units because of non-payment never to be enjoyed again. Forget trying to maintain a savings account, putting money aside for retirement, or buying a house. And if you own a house, get ready to lose it.

How Do You know if You're in a Relationship With a Gambler?

Gamblers can't keep a checking account, credit cards, or money in their pocket. Keeping and maintaining a car is a challenge as well.

If you live with a problem gambler, you'll have no permanent residence because you won't be able to maintain your rental or house payments. All of the money is being gambled away. When financial troubles reach their limit you could move as often as once a year.

You may know little about your gamblers' past. They almost seem spy-like. If you meet their relatives they may act cool and reserved. They will relate to you with strange silences as if there is something they want to tell you but dare not.

Chances are they have been drained of money by their gambler and are used to treating him or her with a long-handled spoon. Gamblers do not pay back what they borrow.

Some addicts of this type may have a sense of entitlement and feel that people and society in general owe them something. They have a chip on their shoulders and will always be trying to play the systems society puts in place to get something for nothing.

Gamblers often deny saying things you know they said. This can be confusing. This is because a gambler is a con. Cons always put a grain of the truth into everything they say, but they tell half-truths. That way you can never hold them to anything they say because they will deny that they said it in the first place. There can be so much lying by omission going on that pretty soon you cannot even separate fact from fiction, then - all the things you hold to be true become a blur.

Living with a gambler is a lonely life. Like many abusers they will try to isolate you from family and friends.

If you're with a gambler, stay on birth control if you are a woman, or use protection if you are a man. If you become pregnant, it is better for the gambler because they will want you dependent on them in every way - so that they can drain you. You'll work your fingers to the bone trying to provide for your little ones while they gamble it all away.

Your financial problems may feel like a mystery because you hardly ever see addicts eat a meal, spend money, or gamble. They do these things mostly in private. They often have bizarre sleeping patterns and eating routines as well.

Gamblers play all roles, that of the victim, the persecutor, or the rescuer. Whichever role that will get them what they want.

Caution: You can never win an argument with gambling cons, so don't even waste your energy. Since they are pathological liars - there will be neither rhyme nor reason to their debates - and they can last for hours if you engage them. Believe me, it is not worth it.

Alcohol is a drug. The addict "alcoholic" will never choose love over the drug. The drug won't allow it.

The hidden wisdom - *Do not let your happiness be dependent on an addict's happiness. In a nutshell, that is how one would define co-dependency.*

<>*<>*<>*<>*

<><<<*

Part III. Breakdown – Alcoholics

My Life With An Alcoholic Named Stan.

If you constantly feel like you are your partner's parent, child, or therapist, it is a good idea to enter individual or couple's therapy before this dynamic destroys your relationship.

The third self-defeating relationship I had was with a 29-year-old man named Stan. When my relationship ended with Nate, Stan and I had a whirlwind romance. He was 11 years younger than I, and I fell madly in love with him.

His heritage was a mixture of Spanish and Czechoslovakian. He was gorgeous with thick, black, wavy hair, deep brown eyes, and skin, the color of porcelain. He was slight in stature but freakishly strong. An air of excitement followed him wherever he went and he was very charismatic. When he walked into a room, people took notice.

He was a mountain biker and shaved his arms and legs as some bikers do to help with the **aerodynamics and hygiene** for biking long distances. When he wore his tight biker shorts and sleeveless t-shirts the muscles in his arms and legs would glisten in the sun.

When Stan and I first met, we both worked for the same Sears warehouse in a Las Vegas Nevada shopping mall. I believed that Stan was better suited for me than Nate or Ayden had been, because of his seeming work ethic, intelligence, passion, and energy for life. He seemed to know who he was, and what he wanted. He was going to be the last great love of my life, and we would work together to attain the good life that I'd always dreamed of for my son Bret and I.

We moved in together and then got engaged right away, or so I thought.

Shortly after we moved in together, Stan got fired from his Sears job for clocking in and out for more hours than he had permission to work.

I soon found out that Stan never really intended to marry me. It also became apparent that he wanted nothing to do with being a step-parent. He kept all of this information hidden until well into the relationship.

Of course in hindsight - there are always signs that we admit to ourselves were there the whole time – but that we didn't want to see in the moment.

When Stan's family found out that he had lost his job, his brother-in-law offered him a position in the family business. To accept the job he would have to relocate to Oregon. Stan convinced me to temporally leave my son behind with his father and move back with him to his hometown of Oregon. I was happy to be leaving Las Vegas to chart what I thought would be a better life for Bret and I, however leaving my son behind caused an acute panic within me, and I had a *sinking feeling in my gut* as we drove out of Nevada.

When we arrived in Oregon, I got rehired with Sears within the week. Stan accepted the job with his brother-in-law working as a sales representative for a parts company. He stood to make three times the amount of money than in any of his previous jobs in Las Vegas.

That job only lasted one month.

He had a falling out with his brother–in–law, and quit shortly thereafter.

A few weeks later he got a job at a local airport. It was his dream to work around airplanes. He was ecstatic. At the end of his first week at the airport however, he got fired for running over another employee with an airport cargo vehicle. The wounded employee was only minimally injured; however Stan's lifelong dream of working around airplanes went up in smoke when management found out.

After that incident Stan became sullen and withdrawn. As days went on, his drinking habit increased sharply.

In his youth he had been overweight and had trouble with being teased, so he seemed to be obsessed with keeping his weight down. His food habits became downright bizarre. He would eat only sardines, spinach, and V8 juice in a kind of cold soup. This food combination - along with his beer - seemed to be the trick for keeping his weight down.

He would not allow me to buy other foods. I didn't like sardines, so I was always hungry as a result and would often not have a lunch to take to my job.

Stan's behavior became increasingly unsafe. He would drop cigarettes in bed which nearly caught the sheets on fire. He'd leave the front door to our apartment unlocked or wide open at all hours of the day or night even though we lived on a busy main street in the middle of town.

Stan got his license taken away for a DUI and eventually lost his driving privileges. He was on unemployment and it was hard for him to find a new job. He became overly controlling of the money I made. He would confiscate my paycheck and use the money at his discretion. He wouldn't give me back any grocery or pocket-money.

Over time, our relationship became more and more abusive. Stan began hitting me on the buttocks. At first it was in a fun and flirty way, but then it progressed to an everyday activity, and I was sore. It wasn't funny.

Stan didn't like the way I dressed, but he wouldn't agree on a budget to include buying new clothes. My hair was curly; Stan wanted it to be straight. I was a size ten; he wanted me to be a size six, or he said he wouldn't marry me. He'd make fun of how dumb I was and blamed me for everything that got lost or went wrong.

One night while he was drinking, he didn't like something I said, so he picked me up and carried me to the front door, shoved me outside in the cold, and locked the door behind me. I was in my nightgown but stayed outside for what seemed like twenty minutes in below freezing temperatures. When Stan finally let me back into the apartment, I cried myself to sleep. The next day, I came down with what was being called at the time an "Asian flu." It lasted so long that I had to claim extended sick leave from work.

When I got better, Stan and I separated and moved into separate residences, but I still obsessed after him for an entire year. For some reason I felt as if he was my last chance for a successful relationship. It was as if I were a heroin addict, and Stan was the heroin. He'd give me just a small hit of himself from time-to-time by saying he loved me. That kept me hanging on while he pursued other relationships. Some of these relationships were with married women. It became apparent to me at that point that he was a *player*.

Fast forward - A few months after I left town Stan invited one of these women to live with him. She was kicked out after only a few weeks... pregnant with his child.

Even with all of that, I still *ached* for Stan's attention. It felt almost out-of-body. I had mildly obsessive feelings in the past for my first love Mickey when I was sixteen years old, but never had I experienced such an all-consuming, utterly wretched obsession like this one. I thought about Stan - day and night - every waking moment. I would drive by his apartment just hoping to catch a glimpse of him. He must have seen me because he accused me of stalking him.

Weeks passed by as I sat by the phone waiting for him to call. When the phone would ring, I would count to three before picking it up. I'd try to sound calm even though my heart would be racing out of my chest anticipating the sound of his voice. The possibility that he would invite me over was too much to bear. I was in a constant state of anxiety aching to get a glimpse, a taste, a sight, or a smell of him. I desperately needed relief from the misery I was experiencing from this dark obsession but I didn't know what to do.

If you find yourself in a similar state, realize that you may have what I have coined an "obsession virus." If left untreated, it can do harm to your entire physical and emotional body. It is an addiction and a co-dependency all in one. This illness of the spirit manifests itself as a long-lasting compulsion for the love and attention of another person, who is bad for your well-being. Like many viruses, the longer it is in your system, the more difficult it is to treat, kind of like a bad case of the hives. If left untreated, it can take years to get over. For me, there was only one "Four-Part-Antidote" that worked, and it is described at the end of this chapter.

The Decline

With the end of my third relationship staring me square in the face, as well as being separated from my only child, my emotional health and mental stability were slowly failing. I was in a battle for my sanity. Paranoia and around the clock panic attacks were taking over. My appetite was gone, and I couldn't sleep. I'd suck on peppermints throughout my work days just to keep the dizziness and nausea under control until clock-out time from my sales-support position at Sears. If anyone noticed my behavior, I'd blame it on my blood sugar.

Desperately needing help, I reached out to a medical doctor, a psychologist, and the church. The doctor put me on various antidepressants; the psychologist encouraged me to cry out my problems in the privacy of her exclusive office; and the church, after verifying that I was saved, entered me in a one-on-one bible study class in which I had to memorize dozens of bible verses. Although their work proved to be valuable to me later down the line, at that point in time, it wasn't enough to stop my dark decline.

I received word that my son Bret and his father had become homeless after Nate got evicted from the apartment where they were living in Las Vegas. They moved into a shelter. I pleaded with Nate to let Bret come to live with me - just until he got on his feet – but, he refused. He said he wouldn't let me see Bret again until he was thirty years old.

He was trying to hurt me, and it was working.

To top it off Bret got sick with his first case of chicken pox while in the homeless shelter. I sent a get well basket to the homeless shelter but was going out of my mind with worry. I felt helpless and didn't know what to do.

I needed to rescue my son, but first I had to rescue myself!

Stan came around a few times as I was preparing to move away. One night he made a comment that he'd never leave behind a child of his the way I left my son. His words tore at my soul, and literally felt like he'd kicked me in my gut. He was hitting below the belt, and I couldn't breathe for a minute. He knew how terribly guilty I felt for moving away from my son Bret, and he was using his intimate knowledge of my pain against me. He accepted absolutely no responsibility for his part in coaxing me along the way with promises of a better life for our future.

At that moment it finally sunk in; there was nothing between us, and there never was!!

I felt lower than low. I had left my precious son behind deluding myself into believing that I was charting a better course - basically easing my own guilt - while in reality pursuing a pipe dream with this retched creature. The truth was that I fell out of my gourd in lust and an obsessive addiction to this person. At that point sheer panic grabbed hold of me and wouldn't let go.

It was as if I'd just awakened and found myself in a realm reminiscent of hell.

Thoughts of suicide entered my mind, and I entertained those thoughts as if they were prominent dinner guests at my mind's celebratory banquet. I wrote and mailed letters to all of my siblings, essentially saying goodbye. Then I cracked. It was emotional, mental, physical, and spiritual bankruptcy. I felt myself spiraling into a deep hole.

My Take on Alcoholics

When your world and an alcoholic's world first collide, you won't know what hit you. He or she will often have charisma up the kazoo and will use it to charm you, excite you, and amuse you to no end. An atmosphere of excitement follows high to medium-functioning alcoholics wherever they go, and life is one big party. At least this is how it seems in the beginning.

Alcoholics prefer not to drink alone. If you are dating or living with alcoholics' they will always prefer that you drink with them. You can say "No" to this but expect to be offered a drink about every 20 minutes until you give in.

Alcoholics seem to have a lot of friends, and most people will naturally gravitate toward them. However, you may feel your energy weaken after spending time with a drinker, finding yourself mildly depressed after parting ways. This is because of the adrenaline rush you'll get from being around him or her. When the adrenaline leaves your body, you will feel a temporary low.

Like the sex addict, when you first start dating alcoholics, they will rush at you with all that they have to offer. Their passion and seeming vibrancy sweeps you off your feet.

This is a good time to step back and assess this person you're with before moving forward.

If you don't, you may find yourself moving in with them or at the marriage alter getting hitched. Their passion is alarmingly seductive.

Alcoholics may ask you important questions when you are also intoxicated to try to take advantage of you. Not unlike the gambler, they want to secure a caretaker so that they can spend more time just drinking.

A personal drinking assistant if you will.

Before you know what happened, you may be living with the alcoholic yet find yourself the only one holding down a job, running all the errands, or doing the cleaning.

You may end up single-handedly holding down the fort. It is easy to become resentful at this point.

You will feel your energy being drained by the alcoholic and may be too weak to do anything about it. You'll have been swept up into the addict's world and left with no energy to get out.

Life may become foggy and low quality. It's as if you live with a vampire and *IT* is living from your life's blood. You're in a dream-like state offering the vampire your neck to feed on as if it's a normal way of life. *It's not!*

How Do You know if You're in a Relationship With an Alcoholic?

That question is not as strange as it sounds. Alcoholic behavior is all over the map, and every alcoholic is different. That being said, there are warning signs and red flags, that can be subtle yet recognizable if you know what to look for.

But first – why should you listen to me?

I am not a licensed expert, but I do have some personal experience and background with alcoholics.

- My grandmother on my mother's side was an alcoholic. She used to drink beer from a tea-cup from around 1:00 in the afternoon until bedtime, every day for years. She was one out of three siblings from ten children that had the disease. One of her sisters fell down a flight of stairs to her death at the prime of her life, more than slightly tipsy.

- My biological grandfather on my mother's side was a problem drinker and a playboy. My step-grandfather on my mother's side was an alcoholic, and drank until his death. Also, my step-grandfather on my step-father's side was a severe alcoholic. My stepfather used to accompany his mother as a boy to find his drunken father passed out in the gutter.

-My biological father is a social drinker, gambler, and a playboy.

-My mother and step-father were children of alcoholics, and they were both heavy drinkers at various times in their lives. My stepfather had problems with drugs, shop-lifting, and infidelity, as well; my mother with depression, prescription drugs, obsessive-shopping and mild hoarding.

-My brothers and sister have had bouts with heavy drinking and drugging, as have I. As I look back, I do have regrets as the oldest sibling for setting that example.

-My best friend's mother died an alcoholic; I was engaged to be married to a severe alcoholic; and finally the man I am currently married to has had numerous family - and extended family members - that have demonstrated alcoholic, drug addicted, and/or enabling tendencies.

I feel that all of these personal associations and experiences give me a unique perspective on addiction in general – particularly alcoholism.

So, where were we, oh yes...

When you first meet alcoholics they will put their best foot forward, so you may not detect that they have a drinking problem at all. Many problem drinkers hide the heavy part of their addiction until well into the relationship.

Alcoholics are often obsessive-compulsive. They may be control freaks and want everything done their way. Their moods can change on the drop of a dime, and they are always on the lookout for drinking partners.

They may be selfish and want you to spend your money and not theirs. Some have car accidents and may get their license suspended or taken away for driving under the influence.

Watch your floors and carpeting when your alcoholic is on a binge because he or she may tend to spill his/her drinks over and over again. To be on the safe side, if you have anything of value, hide it. You may catch them wiping up a spill with your grandmother's antique linens. The ones I've been involved with seemed to have no reverence for keepsakes.

It is all-take and no-give with a severe alcoholic. They accept money and affection from you, but as they decline, there may be no reciprocation.

If your alcoholic is the last one up at night or if he/she leaves early in the morning, make sure you lock your doors behind them because they won't necessarily do so.

Some alcoholics have eating disorders as well as the alcohol addiction. They may be bingers, extremely picky eaters, or may not eat much at all. Sometimes they eat strange things like hominy, rice, and miniature baby-food sausages from a jar, for weeks on end. And, these types venomously object if you attempt to keep groceries in the house.

Other alcoholics love to cook, eat, and entertain but may get mean by their third or fourth drink. You'll be able to tell when their tone changes. When that happens, tread lightly.

If you are involved with a happy-drunk, that's all well, fine, and good but after a while, it will be as if you are babysitting him/her all the time. He/she may grab the steering wheel while you're driving, try to make you laugh when you are on the phone with your boss, drop his/her lit cigarette in your couch or bed, laugh inappropriately if you hurt yourself, or somehow take advantage of your insecurities or vulnerabilities, etc.

Often times they'll have trouble sleeping or staying asleep. Sometimes they shake during the night because they are in alcohol withdrawal. They may want you to hold them to calm their nerves.

Caution: When you are in love with a severe alcoholic, you will not be happy unless they are happy. And, they are not happy very often.

Conclusion

A "...Broken Picker..." [1] is a phrase coined by Dawn Masler who wrote the book entitled, *The Broken picker Fixer, From Heartbreak to Soulmate: Finding the Love You Desire in 12 Weeks or Less.* I highly recommend this book to anyone in love with an addict.

According to Masler a "...Broken Picker..." [1] is an inability to pick healthy partners, and if you have a "Broken Picker," you'll choose the wrong romantic partner to love, over and over again. [1] **By being able to** recognize an addict's warning signs, you will be well on your way to mending your "...Broken Picker...". [1]

Note: *If you are hopelessly in love with an addict AKA "PLAYER," you may also be suffering from what I have coined an "Obsession Virus" mentioned earlier in this chapter. If you feel that this may be the case for you, the Four-Part-Antidote below is what helped me to overcome my obsession, and I'm confident it will help you as well.*

"Obsession Virus" Four-Part-Antidote

Part one of the antidote - Get into counseling.

-Once you're in counseling for a while, search your heart. If you are still in love with the object of your obsession at this point, ask him or her to enter counseling for them self, to prepare for couple's counseling with you later down the line. If he or she says "no" get on a jet plane and fly as far away from this person as you can.

Part two of the antidote – Keep a grateful journal.

-Write down in a journal at least five things a day that you are grateful for. When you do this, your depression will lift and your outlook will slowly improve to the point of being able to enjoy humor again. Humor is a bridge to an open heart, and an open heart is a gateway to falling in love again.

Part three of the antidote – Meditate daily.

-When you mediate you will be given the answers you need for your own personal healing.

While meditating one afternoon, I experienced a severe panic attack as I attempted to end my session and stand up. It was so severe that I lowered myself back down to the floor in the same position I was before I stood up. It occurred to me on my way back down that I may have to live the rest of my life with these debilitating panic attacks, and I felt an overwhelming sadness at the prospect.

At that instant I had a vision. In my minds eye I saw my ex (the object of my obsession) and his family all together sitting in their living room. They were viewing a family video, and I was in it. When they saw me, I felt their individual privately-held feelings of love and connection for me.

I knew intrinsically that I would always be a part of them and they a part of me. Then the vision expanded to my being a part of not just them, but everyone and everything on earth. That expanded - from the earth - to the whole universe. At that moment I understood that there was no loss possible. Everything that exists is connected forever.

When that vision passed, I was instantly healed of my severe panic attacks. I went on to have mild panic attacks from time-to- time, but they were far and few between and never again as severe as they had once been. *Meditating reveals and heals!*

Part four of the antidote – Make a list.

-Make a list of all the things you love about the person you are obsessed with and write those on one side of a piece of paper. Copy down all of the things you don't love about the person you are obsessed with and write those on the other side of the piece paper. Be honest, and hold nothing back. No one is going to see this list but you.

Carry this list around with you and read it several times a day, every day. Reading this list will help you to internalize who this person really is in black and white. Your mind will be telling you one thing, but these facts on paper will be telling you the truth. And, facts on paper are hard to reason away!

Now if the good outweighs the bad fight for the relationship. Give it all you've got. If, however, the bad outweighs the good, let that sink in. This may take a while, sometimes up to a year or longer.

Keep this list and continue to read it, until you don't have to read it any more.

When you don't have to read it anymore you have beaten the "Obsession Virus"!

If you still need help at this point, this one universal principle - in particular - was of interest and helpful to me in regard to my own "Obsession Virus" : **The Principle of Backlash** *states that:* "negative psychic energies sent out by an individual and returned to the sender with the same force with which they were sent; occurs when the receiver reorganizes these negative psychic energies as not being his own and silently commands them to return to the sender. [**cf.** PSYCHIC TRANSFER, MIRROR CURSE, SICKNESS TRANSFER]." (2)

If this principle speaks to you, silently command that the obsession plaguing you return to its sender. Better yet, wipe the negative energy off of you, throw it into a candle flame, or place it in a bag and either burn it or bury it. That way it will not return to hurt you or anybody else ever again.

Note: *Then, stay vigilant by studying universal laws and principles, because they will help you to avoid relapse by strengthening your resolve.*

When you are so tired that a hospital stay doesn't sound half bad, it is time to heal your emotions.

The hidden wisdom - *become aware of, and then - protect yourself from - "energy vampires!"*

Note: You'll never get the rest you need in a hospital anyway because they will wake you up around the clock to get your vitals!

<>*<>*<>*<>*

<><<<*

IV EMOTIONAL HEALING

Physical and social abuse affects the emotional life. When your emotional life is traumatized, it affects your sense of belonging, your disposition, and your spontaneity, as well as your judgment and balance. But first, what is physical and social abuse? Greg Enns and Jan Black, the authors of, *It's Not Okay Anymore – Your Personal Guide to Ending Abuse, Taking Charge, and Loving Yourself* [1] define physical abuse as follows:

1. "Destroying your belongings."

2. "Throwing objects at you."

3. "Touching you in ways that hurt or scare you." *(and telling you

not to tell anyone)

4. "Twisting your arm, slapping, or biting you."

5. "Pushing or shoving you."

6. "Depriving you of food, shelter, money, or clothing."

7. "Threatening you with weapons."

8. "Hitting, punching, or kicking you."

9. "Choking or throwing you."

10. "Hitting or kicking you in a series of blows."

11. "Abusing you to the point you need medical treatment."

*Notes from the author Dannie Duncan

12. "Breaking your bones and/or causing internal injuries."

13. "Causing a miscarriage or injuries that require a therapeutic abortion."

14. "Denying you medical treatment."

15. "Inflicting permanent disabling and/or disfiguring injuries."

*16. Playing sex games but then carrying things too far.

"Everyone is different; you may also fill in the blanks for yourself."

Greg Enns and Jan Black the authors of, *It's Not Okay Anymore – Your Personal Guide to Ending Abuse, Taking Charge, and Loving Yourself*[2] go on to define social abuse as follows:

1. "Insulting you publicly."

2. "Controlling your use of money."

3. "Putting down your abilities as a wife, mother, lover, or worker."

*(husband, father, brother, sister, etc.)

4. "Checking up on you."

5. "Taping conversations."

6. "Following you from place to place - stalking."

7. "Demanding all of your attention and resenting any focus on others."

8. "Making a public display of destroying property."

9. "Threatening to hurt your extended family and friends." *(or pets.)

*Notes from the author Dannie Duncan

10. "Isolating you from friends or activities."

11. "Spending paychecks without meeting obligations."

*12. Opening your mail or going through your purse or wallet

without your permission.

*13. If someone calls and hangs up, accusing you of having

secrets.

"Everyone is different, you may also fill in the blanks for yourself."

Laws for Emotional Life

The universal laws and principles that follow as defined by June G. Bletzer, the author of *The Encyclopedic Psychic Dictionary*, are some that definitely helped me to recover from a nervous breakdown, and they will help you as well in your personal journey toward emotional healing.

1. **The Law of Avoidance** states that: "...To refuse to handle a highly emotional unpleasant situation, to deny living up to one's full potential, or to neglect doing something that should be done, will affect the individual's Physical Body, Mental Mind, and lifestyle affairs, through each Incarnation, until one correctly balances with the situation. (Marilyn Ferguson) "Denial is an evolutionary deadend." [3]

An example of applying the law of avoidance:

You are unhappy with your job but are afraid to look for a better one. Then due to stress, you first develop eczema, then bursitis, and finally a bad case of the hives. This goes on for a year until you realize the stress

*Notes from the author Dannie Duncan

you are under at your current job is not worth the physical symptoms you are suffering. So, you find a new job and then all of your symptoms magically go away.

Note: *Not making a decision is a decision in itself; why gamble with your end result.*

2. **The Law of Dominant Desire** states that: "...(Emil Cou'e) "An idea always tends towards realization and a stronger emotion always counteracts a weaker one." Every idea that is formulated in the mind begins on its path of manifestation but all ideas do not come into fruition. Ideas held in the mind with a stronger emotion will outrun, overpower, and nullify the weaker ones, regardless of conscious favorability. The stronger intent or desire in one's mind will manifest a general thread throughout all one's activity. This is the meaning of the "pearl of great price," because the strongest desire may be an unconscious or karmic desire, or the desire may have reservations and bring unpleasant activity into one's life in order to manifest. This law is also depicted in fairy tales in which the subject may "have but one wish." [**cf.** Hold The Thought, Thought-Forms Appendix 2, Emotion, Karmically Desired]." (3)

An example of applying the law of dominant desire:

You have wanted to be a writer since you were a child. You soon give up this notion and think of it as an unrealistic pipe dream, but it is secretly still your heart's desire.

You end up working in a series of dead-end jobs with no real success or satisfaction. Then one day just goofing around, you decide to write a book. The book goes on to become a best seller, and as a result, you are happier than you've ever been.

Note: *Become aware of what you really intend because it will always show up. How you feel is your clue at any given time to what you are attracting. You must strive to feel good. "The Bible doesn't say, "take every demon captive," but "take every thought captive...""* (4)

3. **The Law of Duality** states that: "...(Rosicrucian) "All living situations contain both Positive elements and Negative elements. A positive element by itself does not exist; together with a positive element there is always associated a negative element. Every sound follows a silence; every light casts a shadow. It is duality which gives life to a situation. It is this very duality, the combination of both positive and negative elements, which makes for perfection." All psychics are susceptible to positive and negative vibrations when they tune in psychically. Those unknowledgeable in this work will not know how to tune out the negative vibrations which could bring discomfort and erroneous information. [**cf.** polarity]." [3]

An example of applying the law of duality:

You are skipped over for a promotion at work. You are upset because your family really needed the pay raise. You find out later that the man who got the promotion has a child with cancer and really needed the money as well. You feel sad that you didn't get it but happy for him at the same time.

Note: *We cannot enjoy the positive without the negative with which to compare it; they are two sides of a coin. But remember, when a door closes a window opens.*

4. **The Law of Healing** states that: "...(holistic health, metaphysics) In order to motivate a *permanent* physical or mental healing that does not return at a future time or return in a different form of illness (as a majority of illnesses do), one must correct the cause of the illness. A true healing is to aid in a physical or mental cure and at the same time seek the reason for the disturbance. One must correctly interpret and overcome the traumatic experience at the base of the disease, by a change in attitude regarding the traumatic experience. This attitudinal change erases the experience from one's Belief System and Akashic Records, thus stimulating repair to the body's transceiver point in that

area. The repaired transceiver point stirs up the vital flow of magnetism throughout the Sympathetic Nervous System releasing the obstruction and the body or brain cells normalize and repair themselves. Once the painful trauma is resolved properly by the patient, he or she no longer has to suppress emotions that remind them of that emotional event and the mind or body remain free of illness caused by that particular incident. Original causes can date back from one's past life or past incarnations. Every situation in one's life comes for a reason, and must be balanced with and put in its proper perspective when it is occurring, or it stays with the individual until it is emotionally translated correctly and balanced with, regardless of time. Situations cannot be put aside, suppressed, or ignored without causing havoc in the body or mind until dealt with properly; otherwise, all healings, holistic alternatives, traditional or unorthodox therapies, are only *temporary* cures. [cf. Blocks, Regression, Holistic Health, Curative Education Appendix 5]" [3]

An example of applying the law of healing:

A girl is severely depressed because her parents are killed by a drunk driver. She undergoes therapy for months without much progress.

She decides to visit the drunk driver who killed her parents in jail where he is currently serving out his 10 year sentence. They talk, and she decides to forgive him.

She goes on to become a speaker for MADD: Mothers Against Drunk Drivers and finally has peace of mind. Her depression goes away, and the joy returns to her life.

Note: *For a permanent healing the block has to be dealt with. To heal your body and mind permanently, change your thinking and attitude (forgive) regarding those people or circumstances that have caused you harm on any level.*

Dannie Duncan

I can recall a time in my twenties when I was struggling with the notion of what I should do with the rest of my life. One day in a private moment, as I sat down on the toilet to pee, I began a conversation with God. "God, it's me again. Do you think I have it in me to be a success and to make my family proud? Please answer, do I have it in me?"

Then, quite unexpectedly and out of nowhere, I had this huge burst of diarrhea! It must have come from some dark, secret place, deep in my bowels. It was so powerful that I was sure that I was lifted clear off of the seat and all of the air was sucked out of my lungs! My heart raced out of control and I tried to catch my breath. After a few seconds passed by the situation suddenly struck me as hilarious, and I began to laugh uncontrollably. God's answer was – affirmative! Yes, I had it *in me* to be a huge success... big time!

A few minutes later as I finished my business, I asked the universal God-head "Why would you answer me in the form of diarrhea?" His reply immediately formed in my mind, "You think I can't be funny; I invented humor!"

The hidden wisdom - to lighten up – literally and figuratively!

5. **The Law of Manifestation** states that: "...Suggestion is the generator behind all operations and manifestations in the Material World, and these manifestations cannot happen until suggestion hits the Subconscious Mind and is "taken in" by the subconscious mind. An act, object or event, begins with a mental impression of suggestion in the mind, impregnated by emotions until it is exteriorized; a normal function law is used in Hypnotherapy, Mental Telepathic Healing, Destructive-Brainwashing Cults, and Visualization. [cf. Telepathic Suggestion]." (3)

An example of applying the law of manifestation:

An architect has an idea for a building for a long time until he finally decides to make it a reality. He draws up his plans and presents them to his employer. The plans are approved by his firm and they turn his drawings over to the builder.

Working closely with the architect, the builder is excited as he over-see's his crew build the building. The building now stands on Rodeo Drive in Beverly Hills, California.

Note: *Thought is creative. We are co-creators with God. You can be, do, or have whatever you can imagine. All thoughts create form on some level. Form (or matter) is crystallized thought. Everything you see with your eyes began with a thought, and thoughts will become things.*

6. **The Law of Non-Resistance** states that: "...One can overly desire to accomplish something and keep one's mind and actions on it, constantly. This holds the atoms in rigidity and binds the accomplishment to one because of the strong emotion and activity. One should do one's part as well as one can and then let the plan or situation go, and stop letting it posses one's attention and time; let it unfold and happen; e.g., the little boy plants a tomato seed and, every day, digs it up to see how it is doing, thereby stifling its growth." (3)

An example of applying the law of non-resistance:

Her motto was, "Always a bridesmaid, never a bride" until one day she forgot about getting married and just started enjoying her life. It was then that she met the man of her dreams while vacationing in Bermuda — fell madly in love - and got married.

Note: *If you want something too much, you'll never get it. Don't want it; let it.*

7. **Principle of quickened consciousness** states that: "...The surfacing of stagnant or uneducated energy that is stimulated by a physical experience; outer environmental events frequently occur that at first appear to be negative but result in helping a person express another part of her or himself which they would not have expressed; e.g., the spraining of one's ankle so one will have to stay home from work and read a book that needed reading; cold weather destroying one's flowers, so one has to work in the garden and receive necessary exercise. [**cf.** Expansion Consciousness, Gross Level]." (3)

An example of applying the principle of quickened consciousness:

When he walked up to the airline counter to buy a ticket he was shocked to discover that he had left his money-clip in his other pants at home. He had to miss his flight while waiting for a courier to bring him more money. The female courier ended up being his long-lost high school sweetheart. He decided to go with the flow and postpone his trip until the following day so he could take her to dinner to reminisce. They fell in love and got married six months later.

Note: *When things happen that you do not expect, remember that they might be happening for a higher reason. The Bible states, "And we know that God causes everything to work together for the good of those who love God and are called according to his purpose for them"* (5)

8. **Law of Self-knowledge** states that: "...When one is aware of oneself and has information about oneself, and understands these two combinations, one will have complete control over one's behavior,

making life pleasurable and joyous. The most important kind of knowledge is knowledge of oneself; "Know Thyself." [3]

An example of applying the law of self-knowledge:

He prayed chanted and meditated regularly. Eventually he was able to tap into his higher self and receive streams of information causing him to be in an awakened state.

Note: *Become aware of your self-sacredness.*

9. **Law of Suffering** states that: "... (new-age psychology) All misery, agony, or anguish, whether mental or physical, is caused by FEELINGS. These feelings are caused by one's attitude or point of view, regarding what one is experiencing. One's attitude is caused by one's BELIEF SYSTEM. The whole range of one's belief system results from earthly thoughts in one's first INCARNATION to the present moment. So, one feels the way one thinks. [3]

An example of applying the law of suffering:

A young boy is born with red hair. His classmates make fun of his hair and tell him how ugly he is. He believes them and feels ugly well into adulthood.

The boy becomes an actor and then a movie star. He is adored by women and ends up on the cover of a magazine as one of America's sexiest bachelors.

He now *thinks* of himself as good-looking and *feels* handsome.

Note: *You are who you think you are!*

10. **Principle of Wisdom** states that: "... 1. strength; there is a strength that comes from knowing; 2. the application of Knowledge; Awareness happens first; practice of awareness turns it into knowledge; the correct

and timely use of knowledge turns it into wisdom for that person; this wisdom is then impinged upon the Soul-Mind permanently; e.g., if it is a proper application of a personality trait, one will have that personality trait in every Incarnation from that time on; whatever the situation was that was handled correctly will not occur again as it is now wisdom and does not have to be reexperienced; wisdom is the correct expression of the potential within the human seed, and once learned, will not have to be handled again; (don juan) "a man of knowledge is one who has followed truthfully the hardships of learning; who has without rushing or without faltering gone as far as he can in unraveling the secrets of personal power." [**cf.** Intelligence]." [3]

An example of applying the principle of wisdom :

He continued to choose the wrong kind of women and he was miserable. He finally decided to take a time out. He became celibate for four years and studied everything he could get his hands on relating to love, relationship and soul growth. At the end of that fourth year mark, he met and fell in love with a wise and kind woman. They built a non-profit center together for abused animals and lived blissfully into their future.

Note: *Practice awareness, and seek knowledge. Utilizing the knowledge you discover, turns it into wisdom and your life changes for the better!*

Signs that your emotions are healing are when you feel safe with yourself, and when you allow yourself to live your dreams.

Pitfalls On The Road To Emotional Healing Can Be:

Joshua David Stone the author of *Soul Psychology: How to Clear Negative Emotions and Spiritualize Your Life* [6] recommends avoiding the following temptations in order to facilitate a better life:

1. "Not eating properly and not getting enough physical exercise, which results in physical illness and limits all other levels."

As you neglect yourself, you become vulnerable to energy vampires.

2. "Isolating yourself from people and thinking that this is spiritual."

This behavior may be a form of social-phobia!

3. "Being too attached to things."

If you hold on to anything too tightly, you'll lose it, or at the very least, squeeze the life out of it.

4. "Giving up amidst great adversity (this is one of the biggest traps of all - you must never give up)."

Remember, you can create a new reality at any given time through positive thought, word, and deed.

5. "Reading too much and not meditating enough."

It is possible through meditation to receive streams of information tailored uniquely for you! This is like a book in 3-D written just for you.

6. "Thinking that negative emotions are something you have to have."

You have a choice, and remember, you catch more bees with honey!

7. "Loving others but not loving yourself."

What you give your attention to grows and glows; you deserve good things to grow and glow.

8. "Losing your personal power when you get physically tired and exhausted."

You are the driver of your life; don't let go of the wheel.

9. "Being hypersensitive or being too shielded."

"What people think of you is none of your business." (7)

10. *"*Being too critical of and hard on yourself."

"If a house is divided against itself, that house cannot stand." (8) **(and** **– this is true on every level)**.

Say "Yes" or Say "No" to Define Your Emotional Boundaries

*Say "yes" to putting your self up on a pedestal and treating yourself very well; Say "no" to let anybody else put you up on a pedestal that they can push you off of at any time.

*Say "yes" to enjoy things while they are here; Say "no" to thinking things will stay the same forever because the only thing we can count on is that life is a journey and not a destination.

*Say "yes" to the belief that action speaks louder than words; Say "no" to being blown by the wind of another's idle words.

*Say "yes" to your thoughts and feelings and honor them; Say "no" to anybody that discounts your thoughts and feelings as not important or worth listening to.

*Say "yes" to any person or situation that could inspire you; Say "no" to any person or situation that could expire you.

*Say "yes" to anybody or anything that leaves you feeling more than, Say "no" to anybody or anything that makes you feel less than. The first is from the light; the second isn't. I repeat the first is from the light; the second isn't.

*Notes from the author Dannie Duncan

*Say "yes" to help others; Say "no" to allow others to help themselves to you.

*Say "yes" to keep your own power; Say "no" to letting your power subtly slip into another's hands because you think they will love you more if you let them control you or that things will be easier that way.

Great Teachers Have Expressed Words,

Which Will Make A Difference In Your Emotional Healing:

"When I find myself filling with rage over the loss of a beloved, I try as soon as possible to remember that my concerns and questions should be focused on what I learned or what I have yet to learn from my departed love." [9]

–Maya Angelou

"To love is to recognize yourself in another." [10]

–Eckhart Tolle

"What is My Life Challenge? ... To be myself." [11]

–Deepak Chopra

"What you think of me is none of my business." [12] *(This one is worth repeating again and again)

–Terry Cole-Whittaker

"If your mate lets you know what he wants and you use that information to hurt him, you've got to ask yourself why you are in the relationship in the first place." [13]

–Robin McGraw

"Look at the problems in your life. Ask yourself, "What kinds of thoughts am I having that create this?"" (14)

–Louise L. Hay

Recommended Reading That Will Help You
On Your Journey Toward Emotional Healing:

1. *Wisdom of the Ages: 60 Days to Enlightenment,* by Wayne W. Dyer

2. *The Joy Of Living And Dying in Peace, Core Teachings of Tibetan Buddhism,* by His Holiness the Dalai Lama

3. *God Does Not Create Miracles, You Do,* by Yehuda Berg

4. *From Panic to Power: Proven Techniques To Calm Your Fears, And Put You in Control of Your Life,* by Lucinda Bassett.

5. *The Essential Kabbalah: The Heart of Jewish Mysticism,* by Daniel C. Matt

6. *The Heart of the Soul: Emotional Awareness,* by Gary Zukav and Linda Francis.

7. *The REAL AGE Diet: Make Yourself Younger With What You Eat,* by Michael F. Roizen, M.D. and John La Puma, M.D.

8. Any of the: *"I Am" Discourses* (Saint Germain Series), by Lotus Ray King

9. *You Can Heal Your Life,* by **Louise L. Hay**

***

In one of my therapy sessions I expressed to my therapist my belief that my mother always seemed to put the men in her life ahead of her children. I felt that she was seeking attention from the men in her life that she was never able to get from her own father.

Then I started to cry as it dawned on me that I did the same thing with my child, and for the same reason. When I conveyed this realization to my therapist a wave of embarrassment washed over me as I sat there snot-nosed and trembling.

The therapist admitted to me that she left her children with her mother for extended periods of time while she was attending graduate school. She seemed somewhat saddened as she relayed that memory to me. We both sat there in the privacy of her office communing in our pain.

The hidden wisdom – *They say hindsight is better than foresight; however, when you treat others as you want to be treated hindsight and foresight become equal partners, leading to peace and pleasantries.*

<>*<>*<>*<>*

V. WARRIORS DON'T CARRY BAGGAGE

Childhood Snapshots of Mad Moments!

When my mother was nineteen, she married her first husband Corey (my stepfather). I was three years old. They stayed together until I was almost ten. During their six-year marriage, they had three children – two boys and a girl - that they both seemed to enjoy. On the other hand, their behaviors toward me always left me confused and feeling rejected.

My stepfather spanked me a little too often and seemed to enjoy it. He would make me pull my dress up, pull my underwear down, and bend over the bed before he would deliver the blows with his belt or a wooden paddle that he kept hanging on the wall.

My mother always seemed to be embarrassed of me and hid me from her friends.

As far back as I can remember, I felt as if things were not quite right in my world. When my mother cried or seemed unhappy, nobody seemed to notice but me. At our family gatherings, the men would often abuse the women both physically and verbally. I recall one incident in particular where my uncle slapped his wife around while the other people surrounded them in sort of a circle and watched the beating unfold. They were like a bunch of zombies; there was no emotion on their faces whatsoever. I was horrified.

When I was four years old, we were at another family gathering where I met a cousin for the first time. She was about my age. The adults put the little girl and me in the middle of the room just to see what we would do when we met.

My cousin instantly attacked me and began slapping me repeatedly. The adults seemed to be amused by all of this.

My stepfather's mother - my grandmother - openly chuckled.

I was both astonished and confused at the same time by what was happening to me. It was similar to some sort of out-of-body feeling where I was just another observer to what was happening in the room. Eventually, however, as the pain set in, I began to cry.

My mother finally jumped up and stopped the beating, but I can remember feeling it was only out of embarrassment that I wouldn't fight back.

Interestingly, the same grandmother that was most amused by all of this taught my younger sister to box some years later. My sister's life story is also one of verbal, physical and sexual abuse, and in her mid-teens she would estrange herself from these same adults.

I felt mixed emotions and learned to protect myself by playing dumb with my dad and fading into the background with my mom. This would go on to last my lifetime.

At age eight, Corey's brother (my uncle) molested me while he was babysitting. He warned me not to tell, however I told my mother what happened as soon as she got home from the party with my step-father. It was never spoken of after that. It happened again with a male cousin about a month later.

That time I didn't tell.

Years later as an adult I would regret that decision not to tell when I'd find out that this cousin did the same thing to an extended family member who was younger than me. If I had told, I might have prevented that little one from being taken advantage of as I was.

My mom divorced Corey when I was nine because of his emotional and physical abusiveness. She met and moved in with a man named Lenny just before my tenth birthday. My mother and Lenny had a very tumultuous relationship.   He was constantly having affairs and abandoning the family after breakups.

Not much time passed before my mother took an overdose of pills prompted by Lenny's unfaithfulness. But she had a change of heart at the last-minute and called her boyfriend's sister-in-law to take her to the emergency room to have her stomach pumped.

 When she came home from the hospital, I expressed my earnest fear of losing her and pleaded with her to never do it again. She agreed but,

I felt an internal shift from open and trusting to suspicious and moody.

In spite of their problems my mother and Lenny eventually married.

Identity Crisis

A few years later, a friend and I were running through the sprinklers on her parents' front lawn. It was a hot summer day; we were both in our bathing suits. The neighbor lady across the street got offended by her husband and son's goggling at our firm young bodies glistening in the sun, through their living room window.

When she'd had enough, she rudely screamed across the street, "Your mother should keep your black ass at home." Since my best friend was blonde with green eyes, I knew she was referring to me. Her husband and son looked humiliated.

I just stood there staring across the street.

At first, I didn't understand why she had made that comment. Then it occurred to me that I had never met, nor even seen a picture of my birth father, and my mother never once mentioned to me what my ethnicity was.

I had always felt disconnected from my stepfathers and different from my nuclear family. The lady's comment woke me up.

I rushed home and asked my mother if I was mixed with black.

She became silent, and then said, "No." Grasping at straws I asked, "Am I part Mexican?" She replied, "Yes." This seemed reasonable to me because I looked similar to some of my Mexican friends. I wanted to believe her because I needed desperately to fit in somewhere, yet I could sense she was lying.

She seemed so fearful that I didn't push the issue.

My mother's anxiety was palpable, and I sensed that it was only a matter of time before her panic became mine.

Peers introduced me to drugs and alcohol at the tender age of eleven and a half years old, and I found that at least at the beginning, self-medicating kept my panic at bay.

Four and a half years later when I turned sixteen, I walked in during a fight between my parents in which my stepfather **Lenny** was angrily insisting that my mother tell me something.

She was pale and silent, and looked terrified.

He turned to me and said, "Do you know what your mother did? She slept with a black man!"

Everything was moving in slow motion, and they were both staring at me like I was a specimen under a microscope. I was aware that they were trying to hurt each other, but the truth was out; I was half black. They were obviously ashamed of that fact, and were using the information as some sort of an emotional chess game between the two of them – however – I felt a mixture of guilt and shame by default.

The fact that my parents wanted to hide the black part of me hurt me yet at the same time I felt responsible for the burden they carried. The shame that both sets of families felt at my birth transferred to my mother and now to me. There was nothing I could do to take away her shame. I couldn't change my skin color. I knew that same shame would be passed down to my future children unless I stopped it, and I wasn't sure I could. I felt as if I was between a rock and a hard place, and that made me angry. I pushed that anger down into a private place, and thought it would stay there. It eventually resurfaced having transmuted into anxiety and depression, and then wreaked havoc in my life.

Anger is a low-level emotion that causes a lot of damage if left to fester and brew; if you can, it is best to nip it in the bud by practicing forgiveness before it takes root.

The next day, my mother instructed me to tell people that I was part Portuguese and part Hawaiian; she and her mother, my grandmother, came up with that story before I was born. The plan hurt me emotionally. I began the lie the next day.

I was officially in the closet.

A few days later, I broke up with my Caucasian boyfriend Mickey. He was my first love, and it broke my heart. But somehow - by breaking up with him - I felt as if I was protecting him from my identity crisis. I was also protecting myself from possible rejection if he felt ashamed of my ethnicity, as my family seemed to.

The Proposition

Later that week in Spanish class, I was asked to stay after school. The teacher sat with me on a bench outside the classrooms. He talked to me about nothing in particular. He would just ask me random questions. He asked me if I was Puerto Rican. When I said no and awkwardly lied - telling him I was Portuguese and Hawaiian – he seemed surprised and acted as if he didn't believe me. His reaction embarrassed me, and I wondered why he was so interested in my ethnicity. These strange exchanges took place daily for about a week.

I was confused as to what I'd done wrong.

He finally told me of a dream he'd had. He said that in the dream I was babysitting for him and his wife, while they went to a school game. In the middle of the game he gave his wife an excuse and came home to see me.

There was a pregnant pause.

I realized he was propositioning me. I told him that I wasn't interested. He asked me not to tell anyone or he'd lose his tenure.

He gave me a D- for the class that stayed on my high-school transcripts.

A few weeks later while walking through the quad at my high school - I had no memory of how I'd gotten there - it was as if I'd just wakened up. I was in a haze and felt groggy. The kids passing me by were staring at what seemed to be my blouse. I got the sense that it was unbuttoned, but I was too paralyzed with fear to look down and fix it.

It was early afternoon, but there was no memory of that morning and I had no idea of how I had gotten to school that day or what happened to the missing time. I had never felt so vulnerable and out of control. It remained a mystery.

A Faulty Father Figure

At home, my stepfather, Lenny, began jiggling the bedroom or bathroom doors anytime that I was changing or bathing. Sometimes he would just crack open my bedroom door quietly peeking in until I'd spot him, then he'd laugh wildly as he marched down the hallway.

I believe his behavior was prompted by a conversation between him and me, when he told me that he had seen me doing something. He wouldn't say what. He had a weird look on his face.

I asked him if I'd picked my nose, or farted, etc.. He kept saying, "No," so I gave up.

I had started masturbating shortly after being molested by my uncle at the age of eight. The molestation woke my body up to premature feelings of sexuality that I didn't fully understand. It occurred to me later that maybe my stepfather had seen me masturbating. When I figured that out, I was mortified.

Lenny never admitted to me that he'd seen me masturbating, but in my mind, it was the only thing that made sense of his illicit behavior, constantly trying to catch me in compromising positions.

I'd complain, but the voyeurism and inappropriate laughter continued.

I became withdrawn and stayed in my room more and more. When I'd come out Lenny would chant "Look, the monkey came out of her cage!" My little brother Ethan began to mimic him. They would do it together, and it became a ritual.

I didn't hold it against Ethan because I knew he was just trying to be like his stepfather, but I switched to dressing in the closet and wearing baggy clothes. I'd binge on peanut butter sandwiches and I put on weight. I was uncomfortable with my body image and developed a phobia of being touched.

I became defensive with adult male family members.

My stepfather's brother, one of my favorite uncles, tried to hug me once, and I jumped as if he was touching burnt skin. I remember the disappointed look on his face, and I was ashamed at my reaction. However, I secretly harbored the false notion that men in general were sexual predators.

Subconsciously Desperate For Positive Male Attention

At sixteen I entered the dating world unprepared with no healthy boundaries in place and only a brief conversation with my mother about birth control. There was no talk of love, mutual respect, or relationship.

By seventeen, I was sexually assaulted while on a date with Tom, who I thought was a friend.

While driving me home after going to the movies, Tom said that we needed to stop by his house to give his dad something. When we got there, he asked me to come in with him. **I said no, but he insisted.**

My instincts were on alert, but I ignored them.

Once inside, his dad wasn't there and I found that his dad hadn't been there before I'd gotten there, either. Tom wanted sex – and I could tell - he wasn't going to take no for an answer. I talked him into oral sex instead.

I was a virgin and didn't want my first intercourse experience to be ugly. Tom insisted that I not cry and then seemed satisfied when I told him, "I am too mad to cry!"

When it was over, he allowed me to leave but - he was high on cocaine so - he told me to drive his truck home. I felt sick that I'd see him the next day when he'd come to pick it up.

The next day when Tom came for his truck, I was peeking through our curtained window. My stomach was in knots. I had a mixed bag of feelings including shame, sadness, panic and relief. I stood there frozen at the window watching through the curtains as he got out of his friend's car and climbed into his truck.

My stomach calmed as he drove off.

A couple of days later, Tom called me with a vulnerable tone in his voice. He spoke with a sense of urgency and said that he wanted to see me again.

He said he <u>needed</u> me! Those were the magic words.

Since we had been school friends prior to the incident, I thought that he might be sorry for what he did and realize that he cared for me after all.

Even at that young age, I was a romantic. My favorite movie was *Romeo and Juliet*. My imagination took over…, and with another lapse in judgment, I said, "OK". When I got to his house, there was no apology, no romantic overture, nothing like I had imagined.

The fantasy bubble burst when he robotically asked me for another blow job.

I was outside of my body seeing myself kneeling there beside someone who had just sexually assaulted me two days prior, and I'd come back for more.

When it was over, Tom asked me if there was anything he could do for me. From a desperately lonely place I was screaming *"Yes"* on the inside! Because in spite of what was happening, I insanely yearned for Tom to hold me, love me, want me, and commit to me…something, ANYTHING! But when I opened my mouth, all that came out was…a pathetic "No."

I was a freshly punctured balloon with all the air swiftly whooshing out of me.

As I left Tom's house, *I realized that I was so forlorn, lonely and insecure that I tried to get loving attention from my assailant.*

In that humiliatingly private moment in time…, I felt like a cigarette butt stuck in thick, rancid syrup at the bottom of two flat ounces of color-drained soda.

I became deeply depressed and desperately lonely.

I kept it to myself.

Three days after my eighteenth birthday, I moved out of my parents' home and into the world. I was *ripe* for the *picking* from any abuser that happened to be waiting out there for a - sad, lonely, immature - young woman, with extremely low self-esteem.

I carried a full load of emotional, mental, physical, and spiritual baggage. I projected that for the next thirty years.

In Hindsight!

My parents' upbringings were not a picnic either, that's another book! They eventually went on to have a change-of-life baby boy together when I was in my mid-twenties and had long since left the nest. When their son reached his teens they separated and our mother moved across the country from California to Georgia with my half-brother. At that point all of us older kids thought my mother had divorced our stepdad Lenny. We would later find out, while she was on her death-bed, that they never did divorce but just went their own ways.

Who am I to judge?

I loved them, and they did the best they could with what they had.

Sure there were good times in between the bad.

But when I look back over my childhood and wonder how I lived through it all, I remember the people who treated me as sacred when...

*They gave me keepsakes.
*They trusted my judgment.
*They laughed with me and not at me.
*They stood up for me.
* They gave me an encouraging word when others were taunting me.
*They looked me in the eyes when they spoke to me.
*They seemed genuinely interested in what I had to say.
*They told me of other lands far away.
*They brainstormed with me for answers to my problems.
*They shared their wisdom with me.
*They trusted me with their secrets.
*They mirrored my beauty back to me.

And, I realize how lucky I was!

They say it takes a village to raise a child, yet it only takes one or two twisted individuals to screw one up. Whether or not you have children, people like *"you"* and "I" counterbalance the rest of the bad apples. We can make the difference in a child's life.

It doesn't take much to make a positive impact on a little one. Those few kind words or actions can change everything. They can truly turn children into little *Warriors, and Warriors don't carry baggage.*

Kids are precious and our future. When you treat them as sacred, they *will* pay it forward!

Dannie Duncan

In the school of hard knocks, students learn life-lessons the hard way. But, when they need to, they can pull from these lessons to save others.

Upon completion, hard-knock graduates are more intuitive than most and are experts at pulling desperate people back from the edge. In the end they will never know how many suicides they've prevented.

The hidden wisdom – *fight, the good fight and never give up, because you are needed in your future!*

<><<<*

VI. PHYSICAL HEALING

Sexual abuse affects the physical Life. When your physical life is traumatized, it affects your trust issues, your inner child, and your ability to give and receive affection. It also affects creativity, intuition, discernment, and your sense of humor. Greg Enns and Jan Black the authors of, *It's Not Okay Anymore – Your Personal Guide to Ending Abuse, Taking Charge, and Loving Yourself*[1] define sexual abuse as follows:

1. "Talking about you or others as sexual objects."

2. "Forcing you to have sex, including sex after a beating."

3. "Criticizing your sexual performance."

4. "Withholding affection to punish you."

5. "Accusing you of looking at, talking to, or having sex with another."

6. "Forcing you to engage in sexual activities that are uncomfortable for you."

7. "Inflicting harm or mutilation to your genitals."

8. "Choking or slapping you during sex."

*Continually trying to catch you in a compromising position, or acting like a voyeur.

"Everyone is different – you may also fill in the blanks for yourself."

Laws for Physical Life

The universal laws and principles that follow, as defined by June G. Bletzer, the author of: *The Encyclopedic Psychic Dictionary*, are some of those that definitely helped me to recover from a nervous breakdown, and will help you as well, in your personal journey toward physical healing:

1. The Law of Illness states that: "...(holistic health) Every physical problem is caused by a psychological trauma which began from a past experience of this life or from a past INCARNATION: and every psychological problem is caused from a physical injury of some kind which happened in a past experience from this life or from a past incarnation. [**cf**. Holistic Health, Past Lives Theory, Reincarnation, Karma, disease][2] ·

An example of applying the law of illness:

She had a severe fear of snakes but didn't know why. When she visited her grandmother she was told about an incident with snakes that she experienced when she was two years old. With that knowledge and the help of a good therapist, she got over her fear of snakes. Incidentally her migraine headaches disappeared as well.

Note*: To motivate a healing, one must correctly interpret and overcome the original traumatic experience at the base of the disease by a change in attitude regarding the traumatic experience.*

Notes from the author Dannie Duncan

2. **The Law of Path** states that: "...What is of worth to one is "his" path, regardless of the hardships it presents, or the length of time it takes.   Each individual has a karmic journey which he or she has chosen to pursue in this Incarnation and he will, somehow, find a way to travel on it.   This road in one's journey will not go to the individual; he or she will go to it if it proves of worth to them.   If it does not, one cannot hold it together successfully in one's dimension of time because it will fall apart of its usefulness.   The direction one should take is within each individual, and only that individual can take that road.   When one finds their "path" they will constantly have an inner drive to keep on it, and when one is not on it, he or she will feel restless and disturbed.   When one finds his "path" one will find security, happiness, and fulfillment from within, regardless of outside circumstances, no matter how traumatic they are.   [**cf.** path Symbolism]" [2]

An example of applying the law of path:

He kept on pushing forward even though everyone told him that he'd never make it out of the bad neighborhood where he lived. He pressed on - in spite of great odds – and not only did he make it out, he went on to become a world-class athlete and millionaire.

Note*:   Clues that you are on the right path are feelings of adventure, passion, joy, love, and excitement, as well as a deep sense of contentment and satisfaction with what you are doing and /or working toward.*

3. **The Law of Personal Transformation** states that: "...(new age psychology) When something new appears in one's life that totally disrupts one's normal lifestyle, one must let go of old patterns, beliefs, mannerisms and activity. The new experience could be an accident, job transference, residential move, new baby, new friendships, a death, etc.. The individual should take on a good frame of mind, and eagerly look forward to the new situation;

otherwise, his or her growth is held back, the atoms stop flowing and the individual experiences ill-health, chaotic activity, and loss of the benefits he or she was to earn from the new lifestyle. The key is to "surrender" and go forth with joy [cf. Holistic Health, Belief System, New-Age Psychology Appendix 5]." (2)

An example of applying the law of personal transformation:

They tried and tried to get pregnant for three years – with no luck. So, they finally stopped trying and went on to adopt a healthy baby girl from China. They got pregnant a year later and gave birth to a healthy baby boy.

Note worth repeating: "… The key is to "surrender" and go forth with joy…" (2)

4. **The Law of Prosperity** states that: "…Anything less than today's need is not enough. Anything more than today's need is a burden and prosperity lies in between." (2)

An example of an effect of the law of prosperity:

She was embarrassed by her meager beginnings. She worked hard and saved her pennies until at last she was able to buy her own house. It was a great accomplishment and she was proud. She thought she had the home of her dreams until she was invited to a friend's much bigger and more beautiful home. She became embarrassed again.

Note: *Rather simple really! If you were surfing you would not want to go overboard or under-board; balance is key in riding out the wave. You get my drift?*

5. **The Principle of Tears** states that: "1. a necessary mechanism in both male and female designed to release stress and to prevent blocks in their systems; has nothing to do with maturity or strength of character; a mechanism to clean out the fears, disappointments, and sadness of one's emotions; 2. (Pir Vilayar Inayat Khan) the waters of the plants of life; an abundance of crying (when necessary) can transform one, as it acts as an alchemical cleanser; 3. white bleeding; tears, allow the hurt to heal from within, similar to red bleeding that cleans out the wound and allows it to heal from within. [**cf**. NEW-AGE PSYCHOLOGY]. (2)

<u>An example of applying the principle of tears:</u>

After she had a good cry, she felt like a new person.

Note: *words worth repeating - "...tears, allow the hurt to heal from within; similar to red bleeding that cleans out the wound, and allows it to heal from within."* (2)

<u>**Pitfalls On The Road To Physical Healing Can Be:**</u>

Joshua David Stone, the author of, *Soul Psychology: How To Clear Negative Emotions And Spiritualize Your Life* (3) recommends avoiding the following temptations in order to facilitate a better life:

1. "Thinking you need to suffer in life."

Think pleasure.

2. "Believing that the suffering you are going through on whatever level will not pass."

"...This, too, will pass." (4)

3. "Thinking you don't need to protect yourself, spiritually, psychologically, and physically."

Other people's negativity can and will hurt you, if someone was aiming a real gun at you, I am sure you would physically get out of range if you could.

4. "Becoming too fanatical in your beliefs."

"Pride goes before destruction and haughtiness before a fall." (5)

Say "Yes", or Say "No" to Define Your Physical Boundaries

*Say "yes" to express your sensuality; Say "no" to allow yourself to be sexualized.

*Say "yes" to place a high value on yourself; Say "no" to allowing anyone to make you believe you're worthless.

*Say "yes" to support yourself; Say "no" to keeping company with non-supportive people.

*Say "yes" to your sense of reality; Say "no" to adopt another person's warped sense of reality just so they'll like or love you.

Great Teachers Have Expressed Words, Which Will Make A Difference In Your Physical Healing:

""Come now, let's settle this", says the LORD. "Though your sins are like scarlet, I will make them as white as snow. Though they are red like crimson, I will make them as white as wool."" (6)

– Christian teaching

*_**_**

As a single parent attending college, I was struggling financially. My part time job only paid $9.00 an hour at 30 hours a week. I couldn't pay all of my bills.

I got a work-from-home job for a chat line. Men would call and the conversations often turned sexual.

When I revealed to my therapist that the chat line job made me feel powerful and ashamed at the same time - she told me that I was going through some of the same emotional cycles and thought patterns that sex offenders go through. Her words felt like a slap in my face, however, when I gave it some thought - I was mortified when I realized that my chat line job was becoming a sick obsession.

The hidden wisdom - To keep from stumbling over the same problem over and over again you need to bring it in to the light of day. Once you get a clear look at the problem - to heal it, you have to feel it. Or, as Dr. Phil says: "You have to name it before you can claim it" [7]

<>*<>*<>*<>*

"Stay in Adventure."

— Ida Duke

You attract and manifest whatever corresponds to your inner state." [8]

— Echart Tolle

"Warriorship is really living your life, not letting it slip by unnoticed." [9]

— Jeremy Hayward

"All this forgiveness offers you, and more. It sparkles on your eyes as you awake, and gives you joy with which to meet the day. It soothes your forehead while you sleep, and rests upon your eyelids so you see no dreams of fear and evil, malice and attack. And when you wake again, it offers you another day of happiness and peace." [10]

— A Course in Miracles

Recommended Reading That Will Help You On Your Journey Toward Physical Healing:

1. *Mars And Venus On A Date: A Guide For Navigating the 5 Stages of Dating to Create a Loving and Lasting Relationship,* by John Gray, PH.D. .

2. *Awakening the Buddha Within: Tibetan Wisdom For The Western World,* by Lama Surya Das.

3. *Sacred World: A Guide To Shambhala Warriorship In Daily Life,* by Jeremy Hayward.

4. *A Course In Miracles: The Text, The Workbook, The Manual For Teachers,* by Dr. Helen Schucman and published by The Foundation For Inner Peace.

5. *What You Think Of Me Is None Of My Business* , by Terry Cole-Whittaker.

6. *Anatomy Of The Spirit: The Seven Stages Of Power And Healing,* by Caroline Myss, PH.D..

7. *Soul Psychology: How To Clear Negative Emotions And*

Spiritualize Your Life, by Joshua David Stone, PH.D..

8. *Bombshell: Explosive Medical Secrets that Will Redefine Aging,* by Suzanne Somers .

9. *The Power Of Now: A Guide To Spiritual Enlightenment,* by Eckhart Tolle.

>>>>>><<<<<<

"Some may be fearless, others fearful, but if thee remain cloaked in love - and warmed by generous portions of passion soup - all humans may rise above these two states and thrive in the tween, prone not to folly nor melancholy."

The Hidden Wisdom — *when you take a chance on love and live life with passion, your life will balance out!*

VII. IDA DUKE

The Encounter!

Shortly before my meltdown, I met Ida Duke, and although it was unknown to me at the time my *healing* journey had begun.

Ida Duke appeared to me in the form of a ninety-year-old woman making a retail return at a local Sears checkout counter in Medford, Oregon. She had a twinkle in her eye, and when she spoke to me, I had the feeling that I should concentrate on her every word. Her advice that followed was to help me thru some of the most difficult times of my life.

After small introductions, Ida told me I looked like a very smart girl and that she had a book she wanted to show me. She offered to give me her home address. I asked for her phone number instead because she mentioned that she was ninety years old - I felt protective of her - and so I didn't want to take advantage of our brief encounter.

She then handed me a piece of paper with the word *cohobate* on it, along with her home phone number. She told me to look up the word *cohobate* in the dictionary, and then to call her when I found out it's meaning.

According to her, cohobating was what she did as a profession most of her life.

I was somewhat drawn in by the nature of her challenge, as its treasure hunting quality sparked a secret enchantment of mine since childhood.

My Search

As soon as I got home, I began my search. I was only able to find components of the word cohobate in the form of *co-ho-ba-te*. These were various base metals of silver, and the like, found in mines surrounded by folklore pertaining to Goblin mischief! *Coho* was a salmon fish. *Bate* meant to reduce.

I finally called the reference department at the local library, and they found the word *Cohobate* in the Old English Oxford dictionary. It meant to pour a like substance over a like substance over and over again thereby purifying the substance.

This intrigued me!

The Wisdom

I called Ida Duke the next day and told her I had found the meaning to the word *cohobate*. She replied , "What does the word mean to you?"

I told her that I thought perhaps she made bootleg liquor in her younger days. I was kidding.

She laughed and told me that my sense of humor would carry me through life. Then I told her that I thought, in her case, *cohobating* meant pouring her spirit and knowledge into someone over and over again, thereby purifying and lifting that person's spirit and knowledge.

She told me once again that I was a very smart girl.

Ida went on to tell me other things. She said, "Love is like water - when you hold it in an enclosed space - it turns rancid and smells. Love, like water, you have to let it go. It will rise up, turn into rain, return to you yet not in vain."

She said not to take anything *too seriously* or hold onto anything *too tightly,* not even her or I'd lose it. She told me I'd go back to school but to not let it go to my head. She revealed that I looked younger than my age because I was part of what she called, *"The Forward Movement."* I was to adventure into aging on the wings of time.

I must stay in adventure.

She Was Gone!

At this point I asked Ida if she was a psychic or something. She seemed alarmed at the prospect, and in a flustered tone said, "No, no, we prefer to call ourselves helpers!"

I thanked Ida and told her she had given me exactly what I needed. She said, "OK," and immediately hung up the phone without saying goodbye. I was shocked - and not ready to end our conversation.

I called her right back, but there was no answer. I phoned her the next day and her line had been disconnected. I inquired and called around the small town of Medford, Oregon to no avail.

No one had ever heard of an Ida Duke.

Did she pass away? Did she ever exist in the first place? I was never to see her again after that, although I still to this day *secretly* hope that I will.

I believe in my heart that she was an angel; sometimes called helpers, I found out later.

Her advice launched me onto a healing journey and continues to support me to this day, as I strive to become whole.

Dannie Duncan

"...To whatever depths one sinks below his or her norm, materially, one can rise equally above one's norm, spiritually." [1]

The hidden wisdom - *always look for the hidden gift in your current situation.*

<><<<*

VIII. SPIRITUAL HEALING

Mental Abuse affects the spiritual life. When your spiritual life is traumatized, it affects your ability to live for today, speak your truth, maintain an open heart, and live without fear. Negative self-concept is also an issue, as well as your ability to care for yourself.

Greg Enns and Jan Black the authors of, *It's Not Okay Anymore – Your Personal Guide to Ending Abuse, Taking Charge, and Loving Yourself*[1] define spiritual abuse (*which I feel includes the category of mental abuse) as follows:

1. "Discounting your sense of right and wrong."

2. "Denying, minimizing, or ridiculing your spiritual beliefs."

3. "Denying your value as a person with legitimate wants and likes."

4. "Questioning your motives for just about everything."

5. "Questioning your sense of reality."

6.   "Refusing to allow you access to worship communities or support groups."

*instilling a sense of shame in you for your ethnicity, nationality, religion, etc..

"Everyone is different – you may also fill in the blanks for yourself."

<u>*Laws for Spiritual Life*</u>

The universal laws and principles that follow, as defined by June G.

*Notes from the author Dannie Duncan

Bletzer, the author of: *The Encyclopedic Psychic Dictionary*, are some of those that definitely helped me to recover from a nervous breakdown, and will help you as well – in your personal journey toward spiritual healing:

1.   **The Law of Emotional Balance** states that: "To balance emotionally is to keep all aspects of one's personal experiences orderly and in the right perspective. This is the KEY TO LIFE. To balance with one's emotions is to make a deliberate choice (regarding an experience, event, situation, environmental stimuli outside personalities, one's own personality, etc.) and feel comfortable, satisfied, and content about the choice. This deliberate choice can be one of anger, or spiritual joy, as long as it is accepted by both the conscious and subconscious minds. The minds decide if it is a pleasurable or educational experience and then put it to rest. [**cf.** LAW OF KNOWLEDGE, EMOTIONS, KEY TO LIFE, LAW OF EMOTIONS]" [2]

An example of applying the law of emotional balance:

After two friends hashed out their differences, one decided to continue to hold a grudge, while the other decided to forgive and forget. They were both content and satisfied with their decisions and continued a relationship agreeing to disagree.

Note: *Have faith that all is as it should be. Treat your emotions as treasured children. On a daily basis see that they are tended to and fully accepted, then put them to bed and rest in gratitude.*

2. **The Law of Environment** states that: "Everything that surrounds you is an extension of one's self. One's home, the furnishings in the home, the automobile, pets, the yard, etc. is a physical picture of one's attitudes, feelings, emotions, and BELIEF SYSTEM. One's environment is the outpicturing of the individual's core beliefs, strong ideas and emotions, about one's own existence, self-worth, cultural blanket belief, and beliefs that were taught as a child. [**cf.** COLLECTIVE UNCONSCIOUS]." [2]

An example applying the law of environment:

Her house is cluttered with too much stuff. Eventually her closet collapses and pictures begin to fall off of the walls. Her car starts to give her trouble. Then she gets laid off from her job. She becomes more and more resentful until she develops a tumor. Eventually it turns into terminal cancer. She dies in a state of despair.

Note: *Your environment is a physical picture of your inner attitudes and beliefs, self-worth and so on. Look at what you surround yourself with, regularly. Is it fun, loving, clean, organized? Is it a reflection of you? What starts inside of you eventually shows up in your environment and vice-versa.*

3.   The Law of Guilt Conscience states that: "(June Bletzer) Guilt conscience is a necessary emotion that helps a person to achieve a higher qualitative life by telling him or her that the activity, speech, or thought they just enacted should not be repeated. A guilt conscience should never last longer than the time it takes to evaluate a situation or experience and make a judgment for oneself... To hold on to the guilt emotion for hours, days, months, or years is self-punishing, self-degrading, and unnecessary. Guilt conscience is an overly worked emotion encouraged by the mores of society. Each individual does the best he or she can do at the time he or she does it because their past acting and thinking has brought them to that activity, speech or thought. Each individual would do better if they could. (Even a planned robbery is the best that person can do at that time.) One minute after one performs an activity, speaks words, or thinks, one can pass judgment on oneself, because one then senses his or her own feeling, the feelings of others in the locale, and the property changes that occurred, which relay back to oneself whether it was right or wrong. But until the act, spoken words, or thought occurred, one could not know the true reactions, and therefore, he or she was doing their best. This law does not excuse a criminal from paying for his or her crime, nor does it take away one's personal responsibility for one's actions, words, or thoughts. Man-made laws should provoke mankind to become more educated, acquire understanding, and strive for good mental health, so whatever one does (which is their best) is within the law." [2]

An example of applying the law of guilt conscious:

She went along with her teenage friends and shunned the girl who was approaching their lunch table - by making fun of and humiliating her - until she turned in defeat and slowly walked away. The look on the girl's face as she sadly left the table haunted her for years.

She ran in to the girl again as a young adult and apologized to her for her rude behavior so many years before. She told the girl that if it was of any consolation to her that she had suffered from the guilt for the last six years for treating her so badly.

As the girl smiled and forgave her, she felt a weight lift off of her shoulders as her long-held guilt emotion melted away.

As Maya Angelou says, "When you know better, you do better." [3]

Note: *Once you pass judgment on yourself, take personal responsibility, and do your best to right your wrong. You need to let go of the guilt emotion. It is highly recommended that you let go of any unnecessary baggage whenever you can. This will keep resentment and its cancer forming energy from manifesting its damaging qualities into your physical life. Then, allow the over-all experience to help you to achieve a higher quality of life, by extracting the lesson and applying it to your next adventure!*

4. The Law of Like Attracts Like states that: "Atoms will colonize because of their similarity, and thereby form various levels of matter. That which has similarity will be in sympathy or be compatible with that of like nature, working both subjectively and objectively; "birds of a feather flock together." No one escapes this principle in this plane or in the ETHIRIC WORLD. Negative and inferior thoughts bring about undesirable and subordinate manifestations. Positive outlook on life brings happiness and beneficial manifestations. This law works through-out all types of PSYCHISM and MEDIUMSHIP. One should start with a neutral mind in order to perceive correct psychic information. (Robert E. Massy) "Nonsense begets nonsense, junk gives out junk and brings back junk." [2]

An example of applying the law of like attracts like:

The angrier and more negative she became the more she seemed to attract angry and negative people in to her life, until she finally realized that this was not just a coincidence.

Note: *If you plant a negative seed, you won't get a positive tree, and vice versa. It makes sense.*

5. A Principle of Wheel of Life states that: (**Dannie Duncan**) "Love is the gravity that holds everything together. When you operate from a center of love (right attitude, and intention with compassion while holding yourself and others as sacred), outwardly - from the inside out - all that you give out will come back to you magnified, resulting in your becoming magnetized (as in Remember). A magnetic personality will give you the ability to draw positive results to yourself. You will be operating under the law of expansion. However, when you operate from a center without love (selfish, or evil attitude, or intention, without compassion or holding yourself and others as sacred) inwardly – from the outside in - you form somewhat of a black hole effect, which results in a demagnetized personality. This ends in all that you want eluding you. In this case, love or gravity will not hold things together (as in Dismember). Things in your life will slowly fall apart on every level (mentally, spiritually, physically, and emotionally). You will be operating under the law of contraction.

An example of applying the principle of wheel of life:

He has a negative attitude and complains every day. His business slows down and he can't pay his bills. He develops a tumor in his neck and has to have surgery. He discovers his teenage son is on drugs. He confronts him. His teenage son runs away. He thinks, "When it rains it pours."

Note: *What you generate as output becomes input. An attitude of gratitude and love makes the difference. Life is a circle, and you get what you give.*

Signs that you are healing spiritually are a feeling of being a part of something bigger than yourself, charisma, less or no - fear of death, reduced attachment to material things, and self-mastery.

Pitfalls On The Road To Spiritual Healing Can Be:

Joshua David Stone author of, *Soul Psychology: How to Clear Negative Emotions and Spiritualize Your Life* [4] recommends avoiding the following temptations in order to facilitate a better life:

1. "Becoming an extremist and not being moderate in all things."

    Too much of a good thing can be a bad thing and vice-versa.

 2. "Letting your sexuality run you instead of mastering it."

    Self-medicating can take many forms; sex addiction is one of them.

3. "Taking responsibility for other people."

    Have you ever met anyone who really wanted you to do that? Taking on other peoples' stuff can be a heavy burden. It's really not our karma to take on and none of our business.

4. "Needing to control others."

    This can backfire and drain the life out of you.

5.   "Being too preoccupied with self and not being concerned enough about being of service to others."

We reap what we sow.

6.   "Seeing appearances instead of seeing the true reality behind all appearance."

We are all made of the same stuff of the universe and we are all here to purposefully create. There will always be people better or worse off than ourselves; we should be grateful for who we are and what we have, observing others without judgment.

Say "Yes" or Say "No" to Define Your Spiritual Boundaries

*Say "yes" to following your own instincts; Say "no" to following someone else's instincts if it goes against your better judgment.

*Say "yes" to any dreams you may have; Say "no" to anyone trying to squelch them.

*Say "yes" to commit to a sound decision; Say "no" to constantly second-guessing yourself.

*Say "yes" to going through any doors of opportunity; Say "no" to not thinking out of the box when it comes to revisiting lost opportunities.

Great Teachers Have Expressed Words,

Which Will Make A Difference In Your Spiritual Healing:

"We teach people how to treat us." (5) "You can't change what you don't acknowledge." (6)

– Dr. Phil McGraw

My mother always told me that I didn't leave the nest, I fell out of it head first. She said that I was my own worst enemy. It didn't really hit home until after my breakdown. I ran across a piece of information describing the systematic use of psychological torture used on prisoners of war. I was shocked when I realized that every bit of what I read in that particular article I had allowed to be done to me, by various abusers over time.

The hidden wisdom - *The earlier a person puts healthy boundaries in place, the healthier and happier a life they will lead.*

"There is a Zen teaching, a koan, "Not two, one."" [7]

— Zen Teaching

"If you cannot detect what is hurting you, it may be that you have been trying to squeeze yourself into a situation in which you did not belong, a situation that you have outgrown." [8]

— Iyanla Vansant

"In any situation in which you are uncertain, the first thing to consider, very simply, is "What do I want to come of this? What is it *for?*" The clarification of the goal belongs at the beginning, for it is this that will determine the outcome. In the ego's procedure this is reversed." [9]

— Course in Miracles

"Men feel cherished when they are needed.
Women feel cherished when they are loved..." [10]

— John Gray, PH.D.

"We refer to that time between your offering of a thought and its physical manifestation as "the buffer time." This is that wonderful time of offering thought, noticing how it feels, adjusting the thought to achieve an even better feeling, and then, in an attitude of absolute expectation, enjoying the gentle, steady unfolding of anything and everything that you have concluded as your desire." [11]

— Ester and Jerry Hicks

Recommended Reading That Will Help You

On Your Journey Toward Spiritual Healing:

1. *Neale Donald Walsch on Relationships, Applications for Living series, By Neale Donald Walsch.*

2. *The Mars & Venus Diet and Exercise Solution: Create the Brain Chemistry of Health, Happiness, and Lasting Romance,* by John Gray, PH.D.

3. Any of the, *Conversations* with *God: An Uncommon Dialogue,* books by Neale Donald Walsch.

4. *A Return to Love: Reflections on the Principles of "A Course in Miracles",* by Marianne Williamson.

5. *Stillness Speaks,* by Eckhart Tolle

6. *Mans Search for Meaning,* by Viktor Frankl

7. *In The Meantime, Finding Yourself and the Love You Want*, by Iyanla Vanzant

8. Any books, videos, or articles by Master Ching Hai

9. *How To Know God: The Soul's Journey into the Mystery of Mysteries,* by Deepak Chopra

My mother – spoken from the hospital gurney in the emergency room three months before she died: "If anything happens to me, you were a good daughter."

The hidden wisdom – *it's never too late to give or to accept a gift.*

<>*<>*<>*<>*

IX. BECOME YOUR OWN HERO

My fiancé left me. I had no friends or relatives in Oregon, and I felt completely alone. I was working two part-time jobs during the weekdays and two more on the weekends. I didn't own a car, and it was the dead of winter.

During the week I'd walk several miles to my first job, which started at 6:00 a.m. and ended at 2:30 p.m.; then even more miles to my second job which started at 3:30 p.m. I got off that job at 10:00 p.m.. I'd often feel nauseated and dizzy as I'd walk miles home in the coldness of night.

Dogs barked as I walked by various houses, and guys shouted lewd remarks from passing cars. Sometimes they would purposely drive thru puddles of muddy rainwater that had gathered in the gutters and **a wave of cold dirty water would hit me.**

I'd hear them laughing as they drove off.

One night after being drenched in such a way by a passing car, I'd had enough. I was simply so tired that I didn't think I could go on.

It was the kind of fatigue that seeps all the way down into your bones.

I just wanted to give up, just lie down on the sidewalk, in the dark and die.

At that exact moment, images flashed through my mind of the ones I loved and were yet to love.

Something rose up inside of me that felt very powerful.

I got a glimpse of my mother and my son, as well as my future husband and others that I didn't yet know. I could feel that they all needed me in my future, especially my mother. There was no doubt in my mind.

Then an image appeared in my mind's eye of myself in full combat gear on the front lines of a war. It was nighttime, and my comrades' lives were dependent upon me to lead them through the dark, smoky battlefield, guns shooting running forward.

It was up to me!

In that lifetime I made the decision that I couldn't give up and let my platoon die.

However, both lifetimes seemed to be happening at the same time. I had to pull strength from somewhere right then. I took a deep breath and the fatigue vanished instantly. It was as if something outside of me was breathing life force into me. Burdens lifted and I felt exhilarated. My energy increased, and I became infused with an enthusiastic determination that was not present a moment before.

In An Instant I Became My Own Hero!

I made a firm decision in that moment to never give up. I didn't really know who in this lifetime I was meant to touch, and change, and love, and encourage, and pull back from the edge. It started with me, I knew it, and others were waiting for me. This was my purpose for being here on earth.

There in the rain - on that *dark lonely street* - from out of nowhere, I was *recharged. I was still miles from home but felt light on my feet as I made my way. It was as if my feet had wings attached to them and I was floating. Then with every thoughtful step toward home I chanted, "Let's do this thing!"*

Dannie Duncan

<u>On Aging</u>

Aging was never an issue for me until my mother stopped taking care of herself. She became depressed, bitter, and negative. She felt that life cheated her, and that aging was a bitch. Her words with me and others were often biting and her tone menacing.

Whenever I was in my mother's company, I felt helpless and desperate under the barrage of her negativity.

Therefore, I shamefully avoided her as much as I could.

I even ducked behind a clothing rack one day so she wouldn't see me when we were shopping in the same department store.

It turned out that she had cancer for a long while and hadn't told anyone.

By the time I found out, the cancer had spread throughout her body, and it was too late to really help her.

She had also unknowingly had several small strokes over time that affected her social skills and communication, which explained her negativity over that three year period and the breakdown of her social interactions.

When I found that out, I asked God to forgive me for having avoided her!

*_**_**

If you strike a match and then try to light a candle before the match gets a good burn going, the match may go out before you can even light the candle.

The hidden wisdom - *do not give your precious energy away to others when you are depleted yourself.*

The last three months of my mother's life were excruciating to watch. She was on large doses of pain medication that didn't seem to help her much, and they incapacitated her ability to fully communicate.

When she did speak, she'd say the words, "Mommy is so sick," over and over again like a religious chant. It seemed as if these words themselves were ushering in her death.

She didn't hold back her terror with me, her oldest daughter, **and** it was horrific to intimately share in her fear.

At one point she asked me to die with her.

It shocked me because I thought a mother would want her child to live on. It saddened me to observe her heartfelt isolation.

In the end, her death absolutely devastated me.

With her passing I was rudely awakened to my own limited mortality. I developed a phobia of aging and death, as well as a disdain for hospitals and a distrust of doctors.

It wasn't until I read a quote from Victor Frankl - a psychologist and Holocaust survivor - that my fear of aging and death dissipated.

The following quote is taken from *Man's Search for Meaning* (1), written by Dr. Victor E. Frankl:

"To be sure, people tend to see only the stubble fields of transitoriness but overlook and forget the full granaries of the past into which they have brought the harvest of their lives: the deeds done, the loves loved, and last but not least, the sufferings they have gone through with courage and dignity.

From this one may see that there is no reason to pity old people. Instead, young people should envy them. It is true that the old have no opportunities, no possibilities in the future. But they have more than that. Instead of possibilities in the future, they have realities in the past - the potentialities they have actualized, the meanings they have fulfilled, the values they have realized - and nothing and nobody can ever remove these assets from the past." [1]

It took a while, but after reading this I came to realize that aging is a beautiful thing and worthy of respect. The good gained from what one has deposited into the past is never lost; it has been treasured forever!

As well, death is a natural part of life. The key to transitioning peacefully is to live ones life with integrity, staying true to who you are and never short changing yourself, so that in the end, although still contemplating unknowns, one is not left in a state of despair.

It also helps to acknowledge the fact that life is energy and energy doesn't die, it just changes form.

Thanks to Dr. Victor E. Frankl's inspired words my acute fear of dying lessened over time, and I eventually regained a healthy attitude toward hospitals and doctors again as well.

Sage self-concept

If you have unfinished emotional business with yourself or another human being, finish it. If the person is already gone, make peace within yourself by speaking the words to them aloud or silently, and then hold on to the highest truth they taught you.

When you torture yourself with negative inner chatter, stop - and then change your thoughts to more soothing and positive ones.

Strive to pursue all of your dreams before you exit here, and then, "on to your next adventure." Question yourself; do you know what your dreams are?

Love yourself first, and chase happiness. If you trip and fall, get up and laugh because, humor will carry you through life.

Know that you are connected to everyone and everything on a deep, almost DNA like level. There is no need to hold onto low-level emotions such as fear, hatred, boredom, or jealousy. You are everything and everyone all at once. You are a spy, a mouse, a millionaire, a tree, an eagle, a beggar, the president, a nun, a rock star, etc. You are in love, healthy, sick, rich, poor, excited, sad, talented, brilliant, deaf, dumb, a dare-devil, everything. And this is so because everyone is connected.

The paradox to this is that you are as unique as a snowflake and the only one here with your own single purpose and ability to carry that out. There are no replacements for you. Your presence is your present. And, as life goes full circle: "in honoring yourself, you honor everyone."

Strive to live with passion, in full color holding nothing back... there is no tomorrow, only today.

Passion can be found –

- *between the spaces and silences*
- *in the doorways*
- *during the dusks and dawns*
- *in barrels of rainwater*
- *by what is not said*
- *looking into mirrors - whether made of glass - or in another's eyes*
- *in the arms of a beloved*

- *where you least expect it*
- *in the pungency of dark bread and sharp cheddar on a cutting board*
- *while peering into colorful pools of water*
- *in the excitement and anticipation of experiencing something for the first time*
- *in the aroma of fresh cut lemons*
- *while peering out the back window at a white washed yard after a full night of snowing*
- *thru the birth canal*
- *dying daily*
- *after a rain*
- *in the sound of water trickling over the smooth rocks of a river bed*
- *in the first smile of a newborn*
- *in the deep giggle of a toddler*
- *while reading a bedtime story to a child*
- *made with your own words*
- *while contemplating a gigantic redwood tree*
- *or watching something beautiful caught unaware*
- *in the moments of remembering – vividly – happy smells and sounds reminiscent of love, and always flowing in a warm wave of gratitude*

Drink it all in without attachment or aversion, letting happy thoughts and happy people quench the dehydration of negativity, for you will tell richly laden soul stories to loved ones while journeying sweetly toward bliss.

Namaste

Note: *No matter what happens in life... know that you have the ability to connect and draw from the universal all the ingredients necessary for a happy life...at any given point in time and space.*

For those who have experienced loss on any level, "...receive the benevolent energy of the cosmos into your own heart and radiate that positive feeling to others." (2) "From your broken heart, you can love and cherish and take care of others, who are your fellow kings and queens." (3)

– Jeremy Hayward

The hidden wisdom *– breaking down can be a form of breaking through, and may promote alchemy. Metaphorically speaking, once you have learned to turn lemons into gourmet lemonade you can guide others to do the same!*

<>*<>*<>*<>*

<><<<*

X. AS WITHIN, SO WITHOUT

Creating a Healing Environment!

After a lifetime of negative self-talk creating pockets of chaos and drama over and over again in your own life, a quest for creating and maintaining a happy, fulfilling, and peaceful environment is paramount.

Yet, you may find executing that quest to be extremely challenging.

Things will slowly began to change for you when you:

- Give love to yourself first.
- Guard your mind and home from negativity.
- Give gentle, positive attention to yourself and to your environment, anything you want to thrive.
- Stay passionate, _grateful_, and excited about life.
- Have a clear picture in your mind of what you want to do, have, or be (visualize).
- Accept the love that comes your way from all sources: people, animals, plants, environment etc.
- Hold no grudges.
- Become comfortable with change and the unexpected.
- And, indulge your creative side.

According to Eckhart Tolle, the author of,   _A New Earth: Awakening to Your Life's Purpose_, one must realize that,

"...you don't live your life, but life lives you.   Life is the dancer, and you are the dance." [1]

Eckhart reveals that it is important to let go of your entire ego's resistance to the present moment at any given time and just be in the day you are in, rather than consistently jumping to thoughts of the past or the future.   And, allowing those past or future thoughts to dictate your emotional state today. [2]

Then ...whatever you experience on the inside today will show up on the outside tomorrow.

Soooo, ask yourself... "How do I let life live me? How can I become the dance?"

You may discover the answer to be that you don't have to become anything...you already are that.

- You don't have to *breathe...life is breathing you*.

- You don't have to *react to aspirations* but *act to inspirations*.

- You don't have to *live with what is already created* but can *create what you want to live*.

- There is no longer *waiting to be happy*...you are to simply *be happiness and therefore no longer wait*.

- *And...always stay in a Heightened State of Gratitude!*

So dive into life head-first and –

- *Keep a grateful journal.*

- *Take naps.*

- *Meditate daily.*

- *Play like a child.*

- *Listen to your favorite music.*

- *Let happy, healthy, positive people into your inner circle.*

- *Only adopt a truth if it resonates as a truth for you.*

- *Play with your pets.*

- *Water and feed some plants.*

- *Sit in the sun, and feel its life-giving qualities sink into your skin.*

- *Eat and drink fresh tasty foods that make you feel good.*

- *Think happy thoughts.*

- *Peek at deer through your window as they dine on the plant-life.*

- *Envision your own success.*

- *Love "love" and draw it into your life.*

- *Laugh with children.*

- *Take an aspirin if you have a headache.*

- *Drink if you're thirsty.*

- *Be kind to you.*

- Buy yourself things you really love.

- Take it easy on yourself by breaking big jobs up into several smaller jobs.

- Save money.

- Spend money.

- Give gifts.

- Receive gifts.

- Email, text, or write letters to loved ones.

- Pamper your body.

- Pamper your loved ones.

- plant a garden.

- Plant flowers.

- Paint a picture.

- Kiss a baby.

- Cry like a baby.

- Laugh often.

- Make others laugh.

- See a rainbow, smile, and then look for the treasure at the end of it.

- Color your hair, colors that make you happy.

- Get down on your hands and knees in the grass, and look for four leaf clovers for over an hour with someone you love.

- Wear beautiful perfume or cologne.

- Make your hair smell good with a deliciously scented shampoo or conditioner.

- Smile with your eyes.

- Share love.

- Feel safe and happy.

- Surround yourself with magic.

- Surround yourself with life.

- Feed the ducks at the park.

- Rub your bare feet over smooth river rocks.

- Breathe in the ocean air.

- Feel excitement.

- Be passionate.

- *Be at home where your heart is.*

- *Dream big.*

- *Heal other people.*

- *Heal yourself.*

- *Be happy for others' successes.*

- *Treasure hunt in more ways than one.*

- *See life as richly decadent.*

- *Be comfortable with change.*

- *Soak in a luxurious bath.*

- *Live in your dream home.*

- *Delight in watching the colorful birds in the backyard trees.*

- *Be a free spirit.*

- *Stretch your body.*

- *Enjoy a good massage.*

- *Appreciate being entertained.*

- *See the beauty all around you.*

- Love it when you make new friends.

- Get your nails and toes done.

- Enjoy being educated.

- Be surrounded by love.

- Show your appreciation.

- Be fulfilled.

- Soar to the heights today that you have fallen yesterday.

- Stay in adventure.

- Adventure into aging on the wings of time.

- Visit the past and future but live in the present.

- Share the gift of you with others.

- Love who you are.

- Be your own best friend.

- See you happy, and see others happy;

and...

- do all of this and so much more today and every today!

The thoughts that you feed to your subconscious mind today, especially thoughts impregnated with emotion, will become your God given realities tomorrow because, *we are our own "philosophers' stone"!*

Now Go Find Love...It's Everywhere!!

And, if you and I meet one day, we'll recognize each other by the -

- Twinkle In Our Eyes
- The Pep In Our Steps
- Our Kind Words
- Gut-level Laughs
- And The Recognition of Our Mutually Wise Hearts. Wink!

Recommended Reading: *The Science of Getting Rich* by Wallace D. Wattles. Available as a free download on www.thesecret.tv at the time of this writing - January 28, 2012: found by clicking the link - gifts for you, then - recommended reading, and then - continue. Scroll down to the intermediate section for the free e-book entitled: *The Science of Getting Rich by Wallace D. Wattles.*

****

"The most important thing in life is your health and human relationships."

-Holocaust Survivor

The hidden wisdom - *An "Ancient Egyptian Saying: "Good health is a crown on a well man's head that only a sick man can see.""* (3)

XI. HAPPILY EVER AFTER IS A STATE OF MIND

When you were a child did your bedtime stories often end with the whimsical phrase, "and they lived happily ever after?" Is part of you still grounded in the hope and comfort that living happily ever after is possible for you? Perhaps you thought you were living in that state, and then it blew up in your face. Or, maybe it has eluded you up to this point – having had your heart-broken more than once – thus causing you to become jaded. Are you waiting for someone to dash in on a white horse and sweep you off your feet? Does it seem that the very nature of "holding-onto-happy" is as elusive as a butterfly?

Happily Ever After is Possible! The Secret: It is as Simple as Picking a Process!!

The "On-Going Life Process" or the "On-Going Death Process!"

The Law of Life and Death states that, "There are two major chemical processes in the body that are always functioning, the "on-going life process" and the "on-going death process." With every emotion, regardless of its degree of feeling, there is a BODY CHEMISTRY change toward one or the other of the processes. One cannot think a thought, or sit in silence, without some degree of emotion, so the body is constantly working on one of these processes. There is no neutral chemical process in the body." [1]

Part of the **Law of Attitude** states that, "Attitude has its degree of emotion and emotion triggers off one's "on-going life process" or one's "on-going death process" in the body. One chooses by his or her attitude which process is to prevail." [2]

If this is indeed true, then it would stand to reason that you are only allowed so many negative thoughts, words or deeds before the "on-going death process" would kick-in .

No doubt this is a bold hypothesis, but what would it mean for you if it was true?

In a nutshell it would mean that your poor attitude would cause negative emotions in you.   If these negative emotions were held in - over a long period of time - they would eventually pour out in the form of negative thoughts, words, or deeds. This negative outpouring would then undoubtedly shorten your life span (i.e. hasten death).

What is an "on-going life process", and conversely an "on-going death process"? A "life process" could be described as a vibrant state of health with all of the benefits that come along with homeostasis.   Positive thoughts, words, and deeds add more vibrancy and life-force to your general well-being, perhaps even boosting your immune system? Concepts of positivity such as gratitude, love, caring, compliments, honor, valor, peace, kindness, support, humor, etc act as a health elixir for your body.

A "death process" could therefore be described as a declining (deteriorating) state of health with all of the negative effects to one's well-being that are the result of a disruption in homeostasis. Negative thoughts, words, or deeds would diminish your vitality, and may even close down your body's natural defenses. Concepts of negativity such as hatred, lies, back-stabbing, cruelty, malice, jealousy, resentment, envy etc., would all be a physical detriment to your health, and may even promote diseases such as cancer.

Question: If you were to conduct a bold experiment in reinventing yourself into an "on-going life process" where would you *start?*

Answer: We live in a world of duality where fear, cruelty, and hatred — verses — love, kindness, and joy. On a scale of zero to one-hundred with negativity being at one end and positivity being on the other, all you have to do to enjoy a better life, live longer, and feel happier, is to tip the scale toward positivity. *To start the ongoing life process: tip the scale to fifty-one percent, and then strive for even higher!*

How do you tip the scale?

Make a conscious effort today to no longer do, say, or think anything in the course of your day that is detrimental or pernicious. If you catch yourself doing so, stop and immediately say or think the phrase, "Positive-thoughts-words-and-deeds." This will remind you to change your thinking.

Then, what ever the situation was that caused you to think such negative thoughts in the first place, mentally lay them at the feet of the mother aspect of God and let her deal with them. Feel the weight of your problems leave your shoulders and relax into that release. Mother's are good at working out the details in life.

When you commit to making this private and personal decision, you will instantly create a new direction in your life towards an "ongoing life process", and your own, on-going, happily ever after.

Is negativity really that detrimental?

I personally observed the destructive power of inferior emotions in my own life during my decline into a nervous breakdown. I also observed how pessimism affected my mother's life during her last three years on earth.

She became cynical and contrary, and failed to take in the beauty of the unconditional love that surrounded her daily. Her attitude seemed to turn her life into a magnet for even more adversity. Some examples of the continual grief that poured into her life while she was in that unfavorable state are as follows:

*The neighbor's across the street began borrowing money from her on a regular basis. She was having money problems herself yet didn't have the strength to say no to them.

*She got laid off from her management position at a fortune 500 company after thirty years of service and was then forced into an early retirement.

*Her car continually broke down and the mechanics couldn't seem to fix it.

*Pictures started to fall off the walls of her home, and then her bedroom closet collapsed.

*Her house got termites.

*She developed pain in her legs and eventually stopped decorating, going out to eat with friends, and shopping, the three things she loved to do the most.

* She stopped reading, which was a life-long passion of hers.

*Her skin started to itch and she didn't feel well.

*Then one day she developed the flu.

*Her flu worsened until her grown children insisted that she go to the doctor, but she refused.

*Her health declined to the point of us having to call an ambulance to transport her to the hospital against her will. The female ambulance worker thought our mother was mentally impaired because the only thing that came out of her mouth - over and over again - were the words, "I'm so sick, mommy is so sick". She seemed incoherent and wouldn't answer any of their questions. The female paramedic made a circular motion with her finger-tip twirling it around her ear, symbolizing that our mother was mentally off. This worker's flippant inference to mother being crazy broke my heart.

*While in the hospital mother told her roommate in the next bed over that she was going to end up as worm-food.

*Mom died less than four months later at the young age of sixty-three from lung and ovarian cancer, a bad gall bladder, and cardiac failure.

Although, all of her five children were there for her during the last years of her life, and especially the last few weeks, her final days were excessively dark.

Some would say that her antagonistic behavior had absolutely nothing to do with her decline - and many would argue that the "cancer alone" caused her demise - and that it was simply her time to die!

But, what if that were not the case?

Consider the following:

*What if it was the condensed state of her resistant thoughts, words, and deeds over the course of that last three years of her life that tipped the scale in death's favor.

*What if she had exhausted her allowable quota of life-long, verbal discordance, so that when that last balky word left her lips, there was no turning back?

Is that such a far-fetched notion?

As someone who personally observed the power that negativity had in my own decline - and ultimate breakdown - I do not believe it is as far-fetched as some would believe.

Negativity is palpable; it's as if you can cut it with a knife when you walk in to a room. It is a shadow covering the sun, a cold chill that overtakes you, or a bad feeling in your gut.

Ask yourself the following questions:

* Have I lived a life controlled by fear?

*Is my head full of perverse chatter that continues day-in and day-out as if my brain is on auto-pilot?

*Do my dreams elude me?

In the bible, Job said, "What I feared has come upon me; what I dreaded has happened to me". (3)

*What do I dread? Am I inviting those things into my life by thinking about them night and day?

What life process am I in?

Make a decision today to tip the scale in favor of an "on-going life process" for yourself!

<u>Signs That You Are in an On-Going Life Process:</u>

Things begin to come together for you in a favorable way.

Friends and relatives stay in touch.

You seldom if ever feel lonely.

It is easy to make new friends, and old friends call you regularly.

*New opportunities show up.

*People are always knocking at your front door, and sometimes at your back door.

*When the phone rings it is a friend or relative, or someone with good news.

*You are invited to events all the time.

*You feel happiness daily.

*Your body feels balanced and healthy.

*People give or lend you money.

*You feel good and have energy to burn.

*You encourage others.

*You feel attractive.

*You have a healthy sex drive.

*You rarely take medication.

*You fill your time creatively.

*Babies, toddlers, and grade-schoolers are in your life, and you love them.

*Your pets flourish.

*Your plants flourish.

*Your life expands.

*Others see you the way that you see yourself.

*You love life.

*You feel like your life is on the right track.

*When you get grey hairs they make you feel wise.

*You don't think about death because you are too busy living.

*You see your glass as half full.

*When something good happens to others, you feel excited and happy for them.

*Time moves fast when you need it to, and time moves slow when you need it to.

*You feel optimistic and grateful.

*You sleep well, and remember your dreams.

*You wake up refreshed in the morning and ready to start a new day.

*You are aware of news and current events (the uplifting and the tragic), however you keep a healthy outlook about the good in the world.

*Etc.

Signs That You Are in an On-Going Death Process:

*Things begin to fall apart all around you.

*Friends and relatives distance themselves from you.

*You feel loneliness often.

*It is hard to make new friends, and your old friends seldom if ever call you anymore.

*New opportunities elude you.

*No one knocks at your front door anymore (not even on Holidays) unless it is a delivery person, and no one ever knocks at your back door.

*When the phone rings it is a bill collector or someone with bad news.

*No one invites you to anything.

*You feel unhappiness daily.

*Your body feels out of balance and unhealthy.

*People borrow money from you, even though you cannot afford it.

*You don't feel well.

*You sleep too much, or you can't sleep at all, and you seldom remember your dreams.

*You complain a lot.

*You feel unattractive.

*You have no sex drive.

*You take many medications.

*You are bored.

*There are no longer any babies, toddlers, or grade-schoolers in your life, and you miss them.

*Your pets die (They may have taken on your negative karma to buy you more time).

*Your plants die.

*Your life contracts.

Others don't see you the way that you see yourself.

You fear death.

You feel like your life has taken a wrong turn, but you are afraid to change it.

Your hair turns grey and it scares the hell out of you.

You see death as a steep cliff that you are slowly being pushed towards.

You see your glass as half empty.

When something good happens to others, you feel jealousy or envy.

Time is moving too fast or too slow for your comfort.

You lack optimism and gratitude.

You feel sad and resentful.

When you wake up in the morning you feel more tired than the night before, and you just want to stay in bed.

You watch the news all day long and become obsessed with complaining about the state of the world.

Etc.

Recognizing Dysfunctional (O'Holic) Patterns in Your Own Life

It is important to realize that when you have been deeply hurt over time, there may be cyclic behavior patterns that crop up again and again causing you to unconsciously draw in dysfunctional (*O'holic*) patterns. You must recognize these destructive patterns and then work toward your own healing.

When you do realize that you need to heal, you may be in a relationship with another person who also needs to heal but isn't ready yet. This could be a parent/child relationship, a friend/friend relationship, or perhaps you are married - or living together - in an unequally yoked relationship. You cannot make that person do anything about it. There is an old saying, "You can lead a horse to water but you can't make it drink."

Taking responsibility for your own healing and then releasing the burden of trying to drag a loved one along with you - kicking and screaming - releases everyone involved, to heal at their own pace.

But remember "Like energy attracts like energy," so when you do heal you will naturally attract healthy people into your life. The unhealthy ones will either begin to heal as well and stay in your energy field with you or fall away because your energies will clash, and it will be too painful to stay together. When this happens - do not be surprised — it is the natural way of things.

The key to healing a dysfunctional pattern is to recognize it, draw it into the light of day, and then to heal it over time. No one is perfect, and I truly believe that *happily ever after is a state of mind.* You gain that state of mind as you embrace happy moments every day, over and over again.

Test Your Waters

You may have heard of the experiments conducted in the 1990's by Dr. Masaru Emoto. "In his popular book, *Hidden Messages in Water,* Dr. Masaru Emoto showed that when positive thoughts and intentions were directed at water that was quickly flash frozen, images of the resulting water crystals would be either beautiful or ugly depending upon whether the words or thoughts were positive or negative. This happened even when words of intent written on pieces of paper were attached to the beakers containing the water." [4]

Human beings are more than sixty percent water (+-). How are your words affecting the waterways in your own body? And, how are your words affecting the waterways in the people, animal, and plant bodies around you?

Enhance your own "on-going life process" by praying for the water in everything, sending loving thoughts to the water in everything, and blessing the water in everything! Remember, you get what you give. Use your own thoughts, words, and deeds as if they were the fresh spring water spraying out from your own private water-well and trickling down over all of life's garden!

Strive to become more than sixty percent Holy Water and help others to do the same!

Then...

COHOBATE, *pour your love and positivity onto yourself and others over and over again, until it resonates within, and permeates without.*

That love and positivity will add up to happy moments, and happy moments are the good stuff of life. And - in the end - it is only the good stuff that really matters. Happily ever after is a state of mind, and this state of mind is, *Your Happily Ever After.*

<>*<>*<>*<>*

Note: Do you have questions like: Why are we here on earth? Where are we going when we leave here? *Dying to Be Me,* written by Anita Moorjani is a must read for the answers to these questions and more. It will leave you breathless and joyful! Her advice is to, "Just express your uniqueness fearlessly, with abandon!" [5]

*_**_**

Stay in Adventure!!

<>*<>*<>*<>*

In the movie - *The Wizard of Oz,* Glinda the good witch explains to Dorothy that she "...always had the power to get home. Glinda didn't tell her before because Dorothy wouldn't have believed it." [6]

The hidden wisdom – *You have the power to do anything, you just have to have faith and believe that you can!*

<>*<>*<>*<>*

XII. AN EXPANDED GLOSSARY OF: UNIVERSAL LAWS AND PRINCIPLES

Disclaimer

Some of the Laws and Principles that follow may be out of the realm of the general public's religious and/or orthodox belief systems or practices. It is not the author's intent to insult anyone, or to repudiate and/or disenfranchise anyone's religious doctrine or beliefs. Furthermore, the author Dannie Duncan, does not claim or disclaim the accuracy or inaccuracy of any of these universal laws and or principles, and therefore assumes no liability or responsibility as a result of the reader's use of any of the information enclosed in this chapter. It is up to you - the reader - to utilize this information at your own discretion and/or risk. Although the author claims that some of the information enclosed, here-in, helped her personally to heal from a nervous breakdown and reestablish her belief in the magic of life again, she cannot guarantee that the information will help you (the reader) in the same or any way. However - with all of that being said - she feels deeply, that it will!

The following universal laws and principles were taken from*: The Encyclopedic Psychic Dictionary,* written by June G. Bletzer, Ph.D.

A1- The Principle of Alchemical Principles: "-1. there is a relationship between total creation and the position of the parts which compose it; all substance is produced from one by the one, so all can be reproduced by one through similarity; 2. process of life or growth goes on in all substance, organic or inorganic, as the universe is constantly expressing its potential, subjected to the law of thought; the nature of the activity of growth follows the nature of thought; to make gold one must start with the thought of gold; 3. there is a force that the mind can control that can act on solid matter ; more powerful than an outside force; sometimes acts instantaneously. [**cf.** Alchemy, Materialization, Transmutation Appendix 4]" [1]

An Alchemical Principle can also be described as "... a spiritual process blended with a chemical process to transform one's own state of consciousness to a higher vibrational frequency by purifications of the atoms in one's body; this is accomplished by first knowing how to transmute lesser metals to higher metals with intense mind control;..." (1a)

A2 – The Principle of Apotropaic Healing Prayer: "-(holistic health) to incorporate in one's method of healing a decree that this healing only take place if the patient has already learned the necessary lessons from this manifestation, if the patient may learn the lessons presented from the sickness in another manner, or if the karmic debt may be worked off in a different manifestation; otherwise the patient will have to repeat suffering to this point in the future; to be used in mental and magnetic healing; a usable simple affirmation: "If it is for his highest good and the highest good of all concerned." [**cf.** Make A Prayer, Magnetic Healing, Mental Healing]" (2)

"...permission should be received before sending healing to another because it could be overwhelming, frightening, or unwanted and will have little effect..." (2a)

A3 - The Law of Association: "– If two or more things have something in common, the "thing in common" can be used to influence or control the other thing (or things); the degree of control depends upon the size of the "thing in common"; the more in common they both have, the more the influence; e.g., eating bread and wine and listening to the assimulated words of The Last Supper, to feel as if one were in the Upper Room. [**cf.** ASSOCIATION MAGIC APPENDIX 2]" (3)

No matter how much you have in common with another person, stay conscious of keeping your personal power; do not let it subtly slip into another's hands.

A4 - The Law of Attitude: "– 1. "Attitude" the only weapon that can harm an individual. Nothing, absolutely nothing, in the universe can harm an earthling except his or her own attitude. No human accident, no loss of a loved one, no natural catastrophe, no personal illness, no loss of property, or job hardship can harm one. It is only the attitude one takes toward these events and experiences that hurts the individual. Traumatic experiences are meant to happen in each INCARNATION. Each experience should be put in the proper perspective, resolved in a favorable manner, analyzed for the good it brought, and balanced with emotionally. Attitude has its degree of emotion and emotion triggers off one's "ongoing-life-process" or one's "ongoing-death-process" in the body. One chooses by his or her attitude which process is to prevail. 2. To whatever depths one sinks below his or her norm, materially, one can rise equally above one's norm, spiritually. One reaches a state wherein nothing material offers any hope and then the SOUL-MIND becomes ready to receive the influx of power and inspiration from the ETHERIC WORLD or the SUPERCONSCIOUS MIND." [4]

Nothing can hurt you except your attitude. Your attitude is your health and life, or your sickness and death.

A5 - The Law of Avoidance: "- To refuse to handle a highly emotional unpleasant situation, to deny living up to ones full potential, or to neglect doing something that should be done, will affect the individual's PHYSICAL BODY, MENTAL MIND, and lifestyle affairs, through each INCARNATION, until one correctly balances with the situation. (Marilyn Ferguson) "Denial is an evolutionary dead-end."" [5]

It is better for your health to handle unpleasant situations as soon as possible.

B1 - The Principle of Backlash: "- negative psychic energies sent out by an individual and returned to the sender with the same force with which they were sent; occurs when the receiver reorganizes these negative psychic energies as not being his own and silently commands them to return to the sender. [**cf.** PSYCHIC TRANSFER, MIRROR CURSE, SICKNESS TRANSFER]" [6]

If you have a negative energy that feels foreign to you, for example an obsession, ruminating negative thoughts, a bad feeling that doesn't go away, an overwhelming fear, a detrimental habit etc., you have the right to command that it return to its sender. Literally wipe the negative energy off of your body, and throw it into a candle flame, or place the foreign energy into a bag and then seal it. Either bury the bag, or burn it, so that the negative energy that you just removed, cannot return to hurt you - or anyone else - ever again. In most cases you will feel much healthier if you implement this universal principle.

B2 - The Principle of Backsliding: "(destructive-brainwashing cults) to rejoin the cult organization after having been deprogrammed; can be triggered by something said, by seeing an old member, or by an emotional event that resurfaces memories of past cult experiences; the ex-cultist then runs away to rejoin the organization. [**cf.** Floating, Sudden Personality Change, Snapping, Deprogramming]" (7)

Backsliding can be described as someone fluctuating "...back and forth between the cult personality and one's own personality after one has been deprogrammed and has left the commune..."(7a) "...Fluctuation will continue until the compartments in the subconscious mind have been completely reasoned with, changed, and a corrected attitude toward the cult solidified...". (7a)

B3 - The Principle of Beating Down Thought: "–to use a word or short phrase to put worldly thoughts and worldly activity out of the mind; used in meditation or as inner-dialogue when disturbed; e.g., "love, love, etc." or "Jesus" or "happy and lovable am I." [**cf.** Mantra, Inner Dialogue]" (8)

"...The sound is designed to assist one to attain higher states of consciousness, evoke Cosmic Energy to manifest within the mediator, dispel disease or create a blessing...".(8a)

B4 - Principle of Bless It: "– (metaphysics) to burst into bloom; to call forth the potential within the seed of a person or object blessed; to sincerely desire that perfection come into fruition for a person. [**cf.** WORDS-WITH-POWER, MENTAL HEALING, SACRED LANGUAGE]" (9)

A blessing is healing and soothing. Remember always, you get what you give.

B5 - Principle of Breathing: "– (esoteric) 1. one of the processes of putting "spirit" into the body, which is absolutely necessary for the life of that body; the master function of the body, all other functions are secondary; the nervous system extracts the "spirit" from the breath, and uses it with an importance similar to the oxygen in the blood; oxygen and carbon dioxide are a secondary necessity; the more deeply one breathes the better one's physical health and longevity will be; 2. deep breathing helps to amplify the psychic signals in the mind. [**cf.** SPIRIT, LOW BREATHING]" (10)

Breathe correctly and deeply for longevity and higher quality living.

C1 – The Law of Center: "- A basic principle duplicated in all nature, giving everything a center from which it obtains its source of energy, intelligence, and pattern which is continually self-renewing. Each center is minutely connected to every other center and to the one Center from which all life is vitalized. (Unity) "Life is lived from center to circumference." [**cf.** MONADOLOGY]" (11)

Our center is connected to all other centers and collectively to one center. (11a)

C2 – The Principle of Chanting: "–an intoning of a chosen sound to accomplish a definite purpose; 1. sound is repetitive in rhythm, uttered in monotone, and varying in intensity and length of time; performed alone or in a group; 2. a spiritual practice of the highest order leading to an inner sound current resulting in a high state of consciousness; enhances the process of meditation, healing disease, harmony among persons, or conjuring up etheric world intelligences for psychic information and psychic phenomena; 3. sensations of heat are felt within the body; activates the kundalini to rise in the spine; 4. chanting increases the coherence and harmony in brain wave patterns; nerve cells are recruited into rhythm until all regions of the brain seem to be throbbing as if choreographed and orchestrated; the two brain hemispheres become synchronized through entrainment; brain wave activity in older, deeper brain structures may also show an expected synchronicity with the new cortex; 5. prolonged chanting: the mind dissolves into the liquid current of energy and becomes purified for the altered state; 6. (Native American, Chippewa) chanting brings life energy down from the sky and up from the earth into one's being; runs through the chakras; gives energy back to the earth mother from the dancers and chanters. [**cf.** Sounds-With-Power, Psychic Healing, Ohm]" (12)

"...Sound exercises a potent and immediate effect on many persons because the right music, pitch, and rhythm causes a temporary vibratory awakening of his or her occult spinal centers; at this moment, a dim memory of his or her divine origin comes to them and he or she is fed by the Superconscious Mind or Subconscious Mind; eg., the Native Americans developed effective sound rituals to control wind and rain..." (12a)

C3 - The Principle of Chi': "–(China) an immutable principle in the air needed for life, taken in by breathing; circulates throughout the entire body making up the twelve meridian lines in the body; this vital force is found in the ethers divided into opposite but complimentary halves and appears in the body as positive and negative areas; see Vital Life Force. **Syn.** TCH'I, QI, Prana, L-Fields, Biocosmic Energy. [**cf.** Yin and Yang, Breathing]" (13)

"...(Vedic) the sum total of Primal Energy from which all mental and physical energy has evolved; manifests in the form of Motion, gravitation, Magnetism, and sustains physical life, thought force, and bodily action..." (13a)

C4 - The Law of Commitment: "– (universal) When an individual makes a "complete" decision, pledging and obligating her or himself to a particular task, thing or belief, everything seems to fall into place, as if the individual was a magnet drawing the correct situations and people to fulfill that decision. "Naming" a change seems to awaken new perspectives. When the mind is "totally" made up to do this or that, and as long as the individual has no inkling of indecisiveness, the atoms will move around working for that individual until that manifestation is complete. Emotional desire behind the decision brings it about more quickly and gives the ETHERIC WORLD INTELLIGENCES an okay to intervene and help bring it about." (14)

If you commit to something whole-heartedly - if it is in harmony with your life-path, and if it does not impinge upon another's free-will - it will come to pass.

C5 - The Law of Continuity: "- Nothing in the universe ever dies, is lost, or destroyed; it just changes form. Everything becomes part of forever. Matter and energy are never destroyed, only transformed or changed. [**cf.** REINCARNATION, ASCENSION, MATERIALIZATION, APPORTATION]." (15)

You can never be destroyed — just transformed. (15a)

D1 - The Principle of Daily Bread: "-(Bible) the "spirit" in the air, the vital life force needed for all things, animate and inanimate, to exist; see Vital Life Force. **Syn.** Primary Energy, Eloptic Energy, Ka-La, Rauch. [**cf.** Soul, Atom, Vibration]" (16)

"... (Burma) spirit, the life energy of a person..."(16a)

D2 – The Principle of Death Process: "- (esoteric) to end one expression of life ready to give rise to another expression of life; an evolutionary step in soul-mind growth, from one completed area into another; (not a set method) similarities: the soul-mind painlessly slips out of the physical body, assisted, if desired, by loved ones from the etheric world who have gathered; viewing a kind of micro-film which shows experiences from the life just passed; seeing a great light, or a tunnel with a tremendous light at the far end (which draws one to it); the soul-mind reaches an ethereal plane level according to its development; a pleasurable, beautiful experience, or an unpleasant one, depending on the accumulated karma, but always physically painless. (Inconcl.) **Syn.** Made The Transition, [**cf.** Death Science, Appendix 2, Law Of Dying Appendix 7]" (17)

The Death Process could be described as "...changing the location of the soul-mind in the cosmos (from a physical body in the physical plane, to an ethereal body in an ethereal plane); an initiatory step on the path of the monad..."(17a)

D3: The Law of Dominant Desire: "- (Emil Cou'e) "An idea always tends towards realization and a stronger emotion always counteracts a weaker one." Every idea that is formulated in the mind begins on its path of manifestation but all ideas do not come into fruition. Ideas held in the mind with a stronger emotion will outrun, overpower, and nullify the weaker ones, regardless of conscious favorability. The stronger intent or desire in one's mind will manifest a general thread throughout all one's activity. This is the meaning of the "pearl of great price," because the strongest desire many be an unconscious or karmic desire, or the desire may have reservations and bring unpleasant activity into one's life in order to manifest. This law is also depicted in fairy tales in which the subject may "have but one wish." [**cf.** HOLD THE THOUGHT, THOUGHT-FORMS APPENDIX 2, EMOTION, KARMICALLY DESIRED]." (18)

Plant your good thoughts and tend to them, until they grow and come to fruition.

D4 - The Law of Dominion: "- (Bible) And let man have dominion over all the earth. The human mind (the interrelationship of the invisible and visible minds) is the instrument that has the privilege to change the vibrational frequency of the atoms, which make this three-dimensional earth and everything that partakes within it. Man co-creates according to the specialty of the THOUGHT and the degree of intensity of the EMOTION accompanying the thought, giving each one full responsibility for the world. This is possible because the intelligence in the mind instrument is connected to the intelligence in the atoms via the electrical system that flows through all atoms. Man can form, make, change, rearrange, and manipulate MATTER in whatever way he or she chooses, "utilizing the laws of nature." Thus each one co-creates his, or her, own type and time of progression of EVOLUTION. Humanity individually and collectively directs the course of the universe with their minds. (Inconcl.) [**cf.** LAW OF CONSEQUENCE, THOUGHT]." [19]

You create your own reality.

D5 - The Law of Duality: "– (Rosicrucian) "All living situations contain both Positive elements and Negative elements. A positive element by itself does not exist; together with a positive element there is always associated a negative element. Every sound follows a silence; every light casts a shadow. It is duality which gives life to a situation. It is this very duality, the combination of both positive and negative elements, which makes for perfection." All psychics are susceptible to positive and negative vibrations when they tune in psychically. Those unknowledgeable in this work will not know how to tune out the negative vibrations which could bring discomfort and erroneous information. [**cf.** {POLARITY]" [20]

Duality allows for a full experience in your life-time.

E1 - The Principle of Eagle: "-1. (Egypt) highly honored bird in many cultures connected with psychism, as far back as records were kept; considered to be a deity; linked psychically with the invisible powers of the sky, sun, and the etheric world in general; 2. (Native American) belief that energy flows from Totality through the eagle; eagle frequently acts as an etheric world guide, giving a person psychic information and guidance; power that emanates from its body, feathers, and claws is held sacred and used for special purposes. [**cf.** Anpsi, Coyote, Deer, Doves]" [21]

"...Animal Psychism; the innate ability that animals have to communicate psychically with other animals, humans, plants, minerals, and other aspects of nature...." [21a]

E2 - The Principle of Elemental: "-(esoteric) 1. a constant, persistent thought on one subject, idea, person, or situation; can be good or bad; thinker gives the thought their undivided attention throughout the entire day; this consistency builds a thought-form, a mass of intelligence so forceful that it can work for or against the thinker, until the theme is dropped..."[22]

Remember that your negative thoughts - held for the long term - can be destructive for yourself and others.

E3 - The Principle of Elements: "– (esoteric) the four basic primary substances belonging to the human being kingdom: FIRE, EARTH, AIR, and WATER; found in every substance known to mankind; each element contains nature spirits and angels who help in the function of the elements, and in their relationship to mankind. [**cf.** NATURE SPIRITS]." [23]

You are inter-dimensionally a part of everything and everything is inter-dimensionally a part of you.

E4 - The Law of Emotional Balance: "- To balance emotionally is to keep all aspects of one's personal experiences orderly and in the right perspective. This is the KEY TO LIFE. To balance with one's emotions is to make a deliberate choice (regarding an experience, event, situation, environmental stimuli outside personalities, one's own personality, etc.) and feel comfortable, satisfied, and content about the choice. This deliberate choice can be one of anger, or spiritual joy, as long as it is accepted by both the conscious and subconscious minds. The minds decide if it is a pleasurable or educational experience and then put it to rest. [**cf.** LAW OF KNOWLEDGE, EMOTIONS, KEY TO LIFE, LAW OF EMOTIONS]" [24]

Make a deliberate choice and then put it to rest. [24a]

E5 – The Law of Environment: "- Everything that surrounds you is an extension of one's self. One's home, the furnishings in the home, the automobile, pets, the yard, etc. is a physical picture of one's attitudes, feelings, emotions, and BELIEF SYSTEM.   One's environment is the outpicturing of the individual's core beliefs, strong ideas and emotions about one's own existence, self-worth, cultural blanket belief, and beliefs that were taught as a child. [**cf.** COLLECTIVE UNCONSCIOUS]." (25)

Your belief system on the inside shows up - in your life on the outside - in kind.

F1 – The Principle of Faint: "- (botane) an action by a plant that compares to a human faint; occurs when the owner is going through a catastrophe. [cf. Watch Plants, Sensation Consciousness, Symbiotic Relationship]" (26)

Some plants are "...believed to have a rapport of integration with their owners since the plants have the properties of being sensors and detectors for the owners..."(26a)

F2 - The Principle of Fairie: "-(Latin *fata;* Archaic *fay,* "enchanted or bewitched") a small, ethereal replica of a human in appearance and mannerisms; desires a rapport with humans but lives in its own invisible culture; a collective word used to mean the whole lower-half of the angel being kingdom of over 1,000 varieties; 1. work with and have charge of the four elements of air, fire, water, and earth under the supervision of the angels; pure elemental vortexes of energy; 2. light energy field capable of forming an etheric body of substance drawn from the etheric double of the earth to carry out its function; 3. live in the rhythm of nature; synchronizes its heartbeat to that of the work at hand; concerned with the process of nature's evolution and it's service to humanity; 4. at times it gives off a luminous reflection and at times it takes on the shape of a human form, altered in size; human form changes with locale; appears in either gender but prefers male gender; body appears loosely knit and felt to have a dense body inside the light body; 5. can be perceived clairvoyantly and seen with physical eyes; cannot be touched; materializes and dematerializes itself going from dimension to dimension very quickly; 6. an energetic vapor-like ethereal substance using the same material that feelings are made of; responds quickly to human emotions; has a sensation consciousness similar to the plant kingdom; posesses the ability of sending a electric charge to stimulate the human intellect and emotions in order to communicate with them; actions and thoughts influence mankind's ethereal bodies; 7. lovable, joyous entity but unpredictable; 8. neither angel nor devil but mediate space between mankind and angels; also spelled faerie, elf, fayerye, fairye, fayre, faerie, faery, fairy, fay, fey, see Nature Spirits. [cf. Nature Spirits Appendix 3 for individual types]" [27]

Some of the names of the different types of fairies are: Air Fairies, Brownies, Cloud Spirits, Dwarfs, Elfs, Field Spirits, Gnomes, Harpies, Imps, Jinnis, Kelpies, Leprechauns, Magical Creatures, Nature Beings, Oceanides, Pick-Tree Brags, Rephaims, Sprites, Tree Spirits, Undines, Volkhs, Water Babies, and Yarthkins. There are over one thousand varieties of fairies. [27a]

*Note: Most people either believe in fairies, or they don't; call me crazy, but I've believed in them since I was a little girl.

F3 - The Principle of Faith: "– (esoteric) 1. to have an automatic understanding of knowledge of a system; a law of function of an entity; perfect knowing; 2. the conscious mind is aware of scientific proof, tangible proof, or its acceptance by the masses, of a certain principle or happening in the outer world; this concept is dropped into the subconscious mind and solidified with repetition; the conscious mind acts accordingly to this belief and it is so; e.g., expectance that the sun will rise every morning simply because it hasn't yet failed to do so, keeps the sun rising; 3. "positive" expectation that "it" will happen and it does; (do not confuse with BLIND FAITH). [**cf**. NEW-AGE PSYCHOLOGY]." [28]

You have faith because things happen – and things happen - because you have faith.

F4 - The Principle of Food Scale: " – (esoteric) foods have been tested for their vibrational rate and then grouped on a scale; scale of decreasing vibrational frequencies shows the following order: fruit, vegetables, seeds and nuts, dairy products, whole grain cereals, fish with fins, flesh food (meat), shell fish, honey and molasses. (Inconcl.) [**cf.** VEGETARIAN, ONIONS, SAGE]." (29)

You are the vibrational equivalent of what you ingest and digest on every level.

F5 - The Law of Free Will: "- Every person has absolute pure freedom of choice every minute of the day. Mankind is never free from decision-making; to not make a decision *is* a decision. Through his or her decisions mankind is *totally* in charge of his or her body and daily experiences. No outside universal or environmental stimuli dominate one's body or experiences.   Therefore, one is automatically accountable for each decision, and this is reflected in the state of one's body and affairs. Mankind has evolved from an instinctual system and is now the only animal in earth with the free will system. Out of man's seven states of consciousness, earth consciousness is the only life in which free choice plays such an important role. One does not fail or fall, nor is one considered immature because one made a wrong choice. If people were not meant to make a wrong choice sometimes, they would not own this system. Choices which oneself judges to be incorrect or un-pleasurable have a stronger impact on learning. Free will is mankind's main tool in each incarnation for learning lessons for evolvement." (30)

Your decisions show up in your body and affairs. (30a)

G1 – The Principle of Gates: "-(Yoga) inner principle that keeps the three lower chakras separated from the higher chakras; will open when the person has given up materialistic thoughts and acts, and is concerned with earning higher enlightenment. [cf. Kundalini, Chakra Lower Man]" (31)

If the chakra's are forced open prematurely - without first preparing through study and meditation - illness can develop.

G2 - The Principle of Gnomes: "- nature spirits made of pure elemental substance, living underground, in mines, and in rocks, absorb the sun through earth and rocks; gnomes have their own homes and government in another vibrational frequency which allows them to pass through stone and rocks easily; usually show themselves about twelve to eighteen inches tall but are capable of elongating and shifting dimensions quickly; gnomes have an energy compatible with humans and unselfishly help humans, urging them to be in control of body health and psychic skills; the gnome brings strength with a flash, and is persistent in his or her good intent to change the human; addicted to mockery and sometimes can be annoying and frivolous in their communication with humans; see Fairies. [**cf.** Earth Spirits, Elves]" [32]

"...a highly intelligent, invisible, formless, powerful energy force working with the etheric blueprints of all nature on earth; capable of forming into a tiny person with differing characteristics, to communicate with mankind." [32a]

G3 - The Law of Good: "– All is good. ALL-THERE IS -is good. There is no EVIL in all the universes, only a system of opposites and POLARITY. There are no tragedies or sin on earth, only an ultimate unfolding of each person. There are hundreds of levels of unfoldment." [33]

You live in a world of duality to gage your good.

G4 - The Law of Grace: "– 1. (June Bletzer) "Motivation," an innate guiding principle that promotes constant change to perfectibility in all things. The potential within each seed of living organisims that motivates it to grow to be a perfect organisim of its species. Grace in mankind is the motivating force that tells one to keep going and do better, no matter what happens to one; e.g., the ability of the body to heal itself. **Syn.** LAW OF PERFECTABILITY. **2.** (Edgar Cayce) "The moment that one begins to forgive himself, he moves under the Law of Grace." When one understands the evolutionary process and the need to be a credit to the universe, one can forgive oneself and go about righting the wrong one did." (34)

When you forgive others and especially yourself you are living gracefully.

G5 - The Law of Guilt Conscience: "- (June Bletzer) Guilt conscience is a necessary emotion that helps a person to achieve a higher qualitative life by telling him or her that the activity, speech, or thought they just enacted should not be repeated. A guilt conscience should never last longer than the time it takes to evaluate a situation or experience and make a judgment for oneself... To hold on to the guilt emotion for hours, days, months, or years is self-punishing, self-degrading, and unnecessary. Guilt conscious is an overly worked emotion encouraged by the mores of society. Each individual does the best he or she can do at the time he or she does it because their past acting and thinking has brought them to that activity, speech or thought. Each individual would do better if they could. (Even a planned robbery is the best that person can do at that time.) One minute after one performs an activity, speaks words, or thinks, one can pass judgment on oneself, because one then senses his or her own feeling, the feelings of others in the locale, and the property changes that occurred, which relay back to oneself whether it was right or wrong. But until the act, spoken words, or thought occurred, one could not know the true reactions, and therefore, he or she was doing their best. This law does not excuse a criminal from paying for his or her crime, nor does it take away one's personal responsibility for one's actions, words, or thoughts. Manmade laws should provoke mankind to become more educated, acquire understanding, and strive for good mental health, so whatever one does (which is their best) is within the law. "(35)

Guilt is a tool to use and then let go.

H1 – The Law of Healing: " – (holistic health, metaphysics) In order to motivate a *permanent* physical or mental healing that does not return at a future time or return in a different form of illness (as a majority of illnesses do), one must correct the cause of the illness. A true healing is to aid in a physical or mental cure and at the same time seek the reason for the disturbance. One must correctly interpret and overcome the traumatic experience at the base of the disease, by a change in attitude regarding the traumatic experience. This attitudinal change erases the experience from one's BELIEF SYSTEM and AKASHIC RECORDS, thus stimulating repair to the body's transceiver point in that area. The repaired transceiver point stirs up the vital flow of magnetism throughout the SYMPATHETIC NERVOUS SYSTEM releasing the obstruction and the body or brain cells normalize and repair themselves. Once the painful trauma is resolved properly by the patient, he or she no longer has to suppress emotions that remind them of that emotional event and the mind or body remain free of illness caused by that particular incident. Original causes can date back from one's past life or past incarnations. Every situation in one's life comes for a reason, and must be balanced with and put in its proper perspective when it is occurring, or it stays with the individual until it is emotionally translated correctly and balanced with, regardless of time. Situations cannot be put aside, suppressed, or ignored without causing havoc in the body or mind until dealt with properly; otherwise, all healings, holistic alternatives, traditional or unorthodox therapies, are only *temporary* cures. [**cf.** Blocks, Regression, Holistic Health, Curative Education Appendix 5]" (36)

An attitudinal change regarding a traumatic or hurtful event is necessary for a true healing to take place. (36a)

H2 – The Law of Holding On: "- Any activity one starts, whether it be a poem, a craft, a home, a love, a job, etc. should be worked at until it is finished as perfectly as one can make it. The joy is in the moments of the making, not the finished product. This law goes further to say that one should hold onto an object or human relationship *only* as long as it makes a learning experience for one. [**cf.** Law of Letting Go]." (37)

The joy is in the learning and the doing, not the finished product. (37a)

H3 – The Principle of Holistic Health Theory: "-good health, disease, life, and its meaning are to be treated as one purposeful unit; 1. one's physical and mental health is related to one's lifestyle, one's attitude toward that lifestyle, one's desire to grow, one's desire to live, and to one's value of life per se; 2. a disease cannot be isolated from one's emotions, state of evolution, karma, ability to balance with life stresses, and one's inner desires; 3. human life is more than the sum of mental, emotional and physical states; one cannot isolate the man or woman from friends, family, job, environment, inner desires, or their attitude toward these contacts and their lifestyle; one must look at all parts together. (Inconcl.) [**cf.** Alternative, Holism, Gestalt Therapy, Fringe Medicine, Mental Healing, Visualization]" (38)

We must look at the sociology, as well as the physiology of a person, rather than just their psychology, to get a full picture of the whole context from which their state of health springs forth.

H4 – The Principle of Holistic Medicine: "-1. any external change in one's life-style or environment, or any method that works for attitudinal change which aims to alter the patient's body chemistry and belief system; should keep the body chemistry altered to the degree of well-being to satisfy the patient's preference; life-style changes include alterations in one's residence, job, friends, living companions, medicine, exercise, diet, pleasures, education, and the release of hidden potentials; 2. anything that is added or subtracted from the patient's physical body, or mundane-activities that helps him or her have a more qualitative life for their desires and needs; 3. (Old English *halig,* "Holy") the reunion between medicine and religion; 4. to unlock a Hold Pattern through various techniques of revealing the past emotional event that was not resolved at the time it happened, and now causes the illness; to reeducate the belief system behind this event so the disease will not repeat itself, or travel somewhere else in the body; 5. To encourage body systems by stimulating the body's own healing energies by "balancing" with emotional stress as it comes along; to encourage efficient interaction with the environment.

(Inconcl.) [**cf.** Blocks, Holism, Symptom Substitution, Wellness, Law of Healing Appendix 7]" (39)

Holistic medicine aims at healing a person permanently, by removing the blocks at the base of their dis-ease.

H5 – The Law of Human Being Seed: "- The guiding principle within each individual that urges one to forge ahead into activity and learning experiences that will enhance one's character and increases one's knowledge. The guiding principle is imbedded within the seed so the seed will unfold into a perfect specimen of a human being. This guiding principle stores in the AKASHIC RECORDS what the individual accomplishes in one INCARNATION to another making each incarnation an improvement. [**cf.** BIO-COMPUTER, CONSCIOUS MIND, AKASHIC RECORD]." (40)

We are getting better and better.

I1 – The Principle of I Am: "-the divine spark of Totality in all individuals; the intelligent potential in the Human Being Species Seed giving the human being motivation to unfold to a perfect human being; a sacred connection with the ultimate; one's true self. **Syn.** Self, Monad, Christ Within. [**cf.** Monad-Ology, Christ]" (41)

"...a perpetual living mirror of the universe, closed off from one another but still sensitive to vibrations of the universe..." (41a)

I2– The Law of Illness: "– (holistic health) Every physical problem is caused by a psychological trauma which began from a past experience of this life or from a past Incarnation: and every psychological problem is caused from a physical injury of some kind which happened in a past experience from this life or from a past incarnation. [**cf.** HOLISTIC HEALTH, PAST LIVES, THEORY, REINCARNATION, KARMA, DISEASE]" (42)

Dannie Duncan

Physical ailments can be helped by healing psychologically – and psychological ailments can be helped by healing physically - your health problems are interconnected. (42a)

I3 - The Principle of Indian Medicine Wheel: "-(Native American) any idea, person or object which comes into one's path becomes a medicine wheel for that person; this object or person acts as a mirror which reflects one's objectives in life and can be psychoanalyzed for that individual; the universe is a mirror of people, and each person is a mirror to every other person. [**cf.** Mantic Art, Body Reading]" (43)

This realization may be shocking to you if the people you are most intimate with are irritating the hell out of you. We must question – what are they here to teach us? In the case that we don't like what we see, we must cultivate positivity within to see a different reflection without.

"...symbols are formed in the atmosphere that precede earth doings and are sent to man to announce or warn of these earth doings..."(43a)

I4 – The Law of Intent: *"-* Intention is the strongest element of every action of conduct. The activity one performs matters little, no matter how difficult or tedious, no matter how conscientious one's efforts, and no matter what one sacrifices to accomplish it. The purpose behind the activity, one's attitude toward the effect of one's actions, or conduct, determines the whole meaning of the activity and determines the result of the action. (Is the activity performed with honest, good, evil, selfish, or helpful intentions?)" (44)

It's not so much what you do per se', but why you do it that matters, and determines the outcome. (44a)

I5 – The Law of Inter-relationship: "-There is a relationship of all things in the UNIVERSE, one to another, whether animate or inanimate, casual or no-casual, because all are constructed of the same atoms, and each ATOM has the ability to remember its past performance in matter before it was dissipated (functions in ASSOCIATION MAGIC)." (45)

Everything is connected and remembered forever. (45a)

J1 The Principle of Jacobs Ladder: "-... 1. (esoteric) the underlying motivating force that drives mankind to a higher state of consciousness; to work toward Ascension to the higher spheres, representing mankind's purpose on earth; 2. (alchemy) a metaphorical representation of the powers of Alchemy; power of ascension through the visible nature; a rainbow or prismatic staircase set up between the etheric world and the earth; 3. (Yoga) the spinal column in a human being; advancement through the chakras; 4. (Unity) step-by-step realization by means of which one assimilates the divine ideas of Truth that come to one from God. **Syn.** Golden Chain, Vital Magnetic Series, Anima Mundi. [**cf.** Imitative Magic, symbolism]" (46)

"...each intelligence, ethereal and earthly, teaches, instructs, and inspires the living chain below itself." (46a)

J2 - The Principle of Jnana: "-1. (Yoga) the incessant focusing of one's mental activity on the desired end result to a problem, without instigating a mental solution, where-by one can arrive at the right solution to anything life tosses one's way; 2. (Vedic) true knowledge of Reality, **Syn.** Visualization. [**cf.** Mental Mind, Thought-Forms]" (47)

Keeping a picture in your minds-eye until "...the picture will eventually become a thought-form strong enough to manifest in the outer world..." (47a)

Note: *Remember, if you are not in spiritual alignment with what you materialize for yourself, you will not be able to hold it in your reality for long before you lose it again. There are no short cuts, you must do the inner-energetic work beforehand (and have the correct intention behind what you do) so that you vibrate at the same rate as your desired outcome, thus allowing you to hold it in your reality for the long term.*

J3 – The Principle of Joy: " – (esoteric) the sensation of PLEASURE regarding one's growth; to accept each experience, whether good or bad, as a step in the process of one's unfoldment and to be content with the outcome as a learning experience; (unknown) "the unfolding of perfectness is the joy of the world." [cf. CURATIVE EDUCATION, ENRICHING EXPERIENCE]." (48)

A key is to be joyful no matter what, it helps to have the faith of a child that "all is as it should be."

J4 – The Principle of Joy Guide: "- a highly intelligent ETHERIC WORLD INTELLIGENCE belonging to the INNER BAND and assigned to a human for one incarnation; function is to bring gaiety to the human, guide his or her lifestyle to balance with recreation and work; manifests as a very young person of either gender; eager to serve when summoned. **Syn.** DOOR-KEEPER. [**cf.** OUTER BAND, GUIDE]." (49)

You have a joy guide that you can summon to help you balance work and play. (49a)

J5 – The Principle of Just Sitting: "- 1. to quiet the mind, quiet the body, and quiet the emotions in a MEDITATION period, with no special direction; helps one deal with controversy in life by not trying to solve it but rather to explore it in a quiet way; 2. (Zen) another name for the use of KOAN riddles where the student is forced to a greater awareness of reality through contemplation. [**cf.** END-STATE, GOING WITHIN, LOW BREATHING]." (50)

All the answers to your problems are inside of you.

K1 – The Law of Karma: "– (Sanskirt) The highest form of justice; begins with a concept that everyone is created equal in the beginning. Each one is completely independent and solely responsible for his or her life and body by their thinking and acting in each life. One governs his or her incarnations, and all the experiences that come with them are from one's own doings in past incarnations. Karma is a system that returns to one, in kind, every act one has ever performed along one's evolutionary scale, showing no favoritism. The sum total of causes makes one's life wherever one is, as the result of his or her own activity and thinking in past lives and this life, bringing one good or unpleasant experiences. At the same time, one builds up from these new experiences for his or her future lives. Whatever energy is expended through thoughts, desires, and acts, a like energy is returned; e.g., "Thou shalt reap as thou didst sow." "Cast your bread upon the water and it shall return to you." **Syn.** LORDS OF JUSTICE, LAW OF COMPENSATION. [**cf.** REINCARNATION, APPENDIX 5]." (51)

The energy you put out there - is like a boomerang; it comes back to you - in kind.

K2 – The Principle of K-Complex: *"-* (dreams) a safety mechanism in human beings that allows them to sleep through trivial noises, no matter how loud, but alerts them to awaken for a noise of an emergency nature; research shows that one chooses the noises he or she wishes to be aware of during sleep; e.g., loud train rumbles will not phase a person who lives near a railroad. [**cf.** DREAMS Appendix 2]." (52)

You have an inner security alarm that is discriminatory.

K3 – The Principle of Key to Life: " – (June Bletzer) to "balance" with emotional stress every day, whether the stress is good or bad: 1. to have the correct attitude toward each experience that life presents, resolving any unpleasant experience at the time it happens; to handle all personal emotions (pleasant or unpleasant) comfortably, intelligently, and satisfactorily in accord with one's belief system; to put each undesirable subordinate or traumatic experience in its proper perspective, integrating it into the whole, as opposed to putting it aside without attitudinally resolving it; unresolved emotions are not put "aside" as supposed, but rather they go "inside" the body, to turn up later in the form of a disease or a chaotic life situation; 2. it is just as important not to repress experiences that are painful, as it is to not dwell upon the activity with resentment, jealousy, condemnation or pity; 3. principle: nothing in the world can hurt a person, no death of a loved one, no accident, no environmental catastrophe, no chronic illness, no loss of job or marriage; it is only the attitude one takes toward these experiences that hurts the person. [**cf.** ENRICHING EXPERIENCE, KARMA, BLOCKS]." (53)

Negative emotions - held for the long term - can and will kill you; switch to positive emotions, and hold them for life.

K4 – The Law of Knowledge: "-The more informed one becomes through formal education and through life experiences, 1. the more understanding one has about oneself and life; 2. the more intelligent one's decisions will be; 3. the stronger one will be in all aspects of one's life (there is a strength that comes from knowing); 4. the more control one will have over the maximum data which one has learned. [**cf.** Law Of Self-Knowledge, Curative Education]" (54)

It is important to "...take charge of one's own well being and practice wellness habits to suit one's desires and needs." (54a)

K5 – The Principle of Koan: "-(Zen, "authoritative") (pronounced "Koan") an unanswerable question or riddle used as a tool for stopping the useless inner Mental Chatter that goes on in the minds of humans throughout the day; forces the students to a greater awareness of Reality through contemplation; the nonverbal and illogical answer cannot be found, so eventually this point-of-focus, over a period of time, breaks the normal inner mental chatter when it resumes; e.g., a koan: "What is the sound of one hand clapping?"; also called Just Sitting. [**cf.** Point-Of-Focus, Inner-Dialogue, Clear]" (55)

Regarding your thoughts as "inner-dialogue": "...sometime, they appear to have no logical purpose; researchers found they affect one's behavior, lifestyle and body chemistry in the same manner as one's deliberate thoughts, due to their repetitious nature, and the emotions they carry; believed to surface from one's present and past incarnations, past and present cultural beliefs, feelings of self-worth and one's values..." (55a)

L1 – The Principle of Lemon: "-(esoteric) a sour, acid fruit that vibrates at the fastest frequency of any of mankind's foods; used over the centuries in physical healing remedies. [**cf.** Food Scale]" (56)

When inhaled, the scent of lemon can alleviate a person's nausea or depression, while at the same time increasing their energy level.

L2 – The Law of Letting Go: "...One should say good-bye without regrets or resentment to anything or anyone that is no longer useful and purposeful in making or adding to a learning experience for one's self (whether it be a home, record, plant, animal, former love, car, a grown child, club membership, philosophy, belief, lifestyle, book, etc.). The pleasure should be in the moment of the doing, the making, or the learning, with the object or experience. This frees one to begin another learning experience without bondage to the old image of one's self. (Don Juan) "One should erase personal history by dropping past friends, relatives, cities, and events; where one has been and what one has done, so no one builds a fog around you or is angry with you." [**cf.** New-Age Psychology]" (57)

Do not be afraid to reinvent yourself.

L3 – The Law of Life and Death: "– (holistic health) There are two major chemical processes in the body that are always functioning, the "on-going life process" and the "on-going death process." With every emotion, regardless of its degree of feeling, there is a BODY CHEMISTRY change toward one or the other of the processes. One cannot think a thought, or sit in silence, without some degree of emotion, so the body is constantly working on one of these processes. There is no neutral chemical process in the body. [**cf.** CURATIVE EDUCATION]" (58)

You are either (fearing) dying or (loving) living – there is no sitting on the fence with this.

L4 – The Law of Like Attracts Like: "- Atoms will colonize because of their similarity, and thereby form various levels of matter. That which has similarity will be in sympathy or be compatible with that of like nature, working both subjectively and objectively; "birds of a feather flock together". No one escapes this principle in this plane or in the ETHIRIC WORLD. Negative and inferior thoughts bring about undesirable and subordinate manifestations. Positive outlook on life brings happiness and beneficial manifestations. This law works through-out all types of PSYCHISM and MEDIUMSHIP. One should start with a neutral mind in order to perceive correct psychic information. (Robert E. Massy) "Nonsense begets nonsense, junk gives out junk and brings back junk." (59)

Similar vibratory rates attract and attune to one another.

L5 – The Principle of Listening to the Skin: "-the perception of things and people through the sensitivity of the skin; a way to see without eyes. (Inconcl.) [**cf.** Eyeless Sight Appendix 2]" (60)

"...a psychic ability varying with individuals and requiring concentration; reports of this study: finger tips and cheeks detect the thermal and density feelings of color; negatives are imprinted on the inside of the forehead; an awareness is felt with the whole consciousness..." (60a)

M1 – The Law of Manifestation: "- SUGGESTION is the generator behind all operations and manifestations in the MATERIAL WORLD, and these manifestations cannot happen until suggestion hits the SUBCONSCIOUS MIND and is "taken in" by the subconscious mind. An act, object or event, begins with a mental impression of suggestion in the mind, impregnated by emotions until it is exteriorized; a normal function law is used in Hypnotherapy, MENTAL TELEPATHIC HEALING, DESTRUCTIVE-BRAINWASHING CULTS, and VISUALIZATION. [**cf.** Telepathic Suggestion]" (61)

Your thoughts + your emotions = your manifestations, in-other-words, the things that show up in your life.

M2 – The Law of Matter: "– (Esoteric) All matter is composed of atoms vibrating at different frequencies made by the constant repulsion and

attraction of electrons and protons trying to balance. The repulsion and attraction is activated by the human mind and emotions and keeps on until atoms of the same number of electrons aggregate together forming the various rates of vibration or matter.   (Jean Chardin) "Matter is conscious energy; mind and matter are one, poles of one continuum. Matter is the human mind in action; there is no substance except conscious energy." (Elmer Green) "Matter is crystallized thought." This law makes all types of PSYCHISM a perfectly normal function. (Inconcl.)."
[62]

Your thoughts and emotions (cause) waves of motion. These waves of motion (cause) a mind-over-matter (effect), which turns these thoughts and emotions into action (manifestation) in the physical world.

M3 – The Law of Meditation: "- When the CONSCIOUS MIND is fully occupied or locked-in on a small focul point for a period of time, the physical SENSES automatically become stilled, and pure THOUGHT or ideas flow from TOTALITY, which could not have flowed with the conscious senses working. Inventors, authors, artists, geniuses, scientists, all receive their new material by becoming so engrossed in their work, it stills outer senses and ideas flow.   Meditation is a deliberate and pronounced holding back of the conscious mind and emotions for a set time, in a particular posture. This allows the PHYSICAL BODY to act upon itself in repair and attunes the conscious mind and emotions to a higher state of thinking, for many hours. Meditation before opening PHYCHIC DOORS will surface higher qualitative information; see MEDITATION APPENDIX5]." [63]

Your meditation provides an opening for your inspiration.

M4 – The Principle of Metaphysical Healing: "-to motivate a "permanent" healing that does not return, at another time or in another place in the body, in a different form; situations, events, and activities are given to an individual to learn lessons and when these are not handled or settled at the time they occur, they cause a broken circuit in the emotional (electrical) nervous system; this is not repaired until that particular experience is resolved and is accompanied by an attitudinal change, regardless of time or incarnation; pressure point areas in which the broken circuit exists will not allow the vital magnetic fluid to flow until mentally-emotionally repaired; any healing, traditional or holistic alternatives are only temporary cures unless the cause is found and resolved. [cf. Law Of Healing Appendix 7, Holistic Health, Alternatives, Meta-Physics]" (64)

There are dozens of unconventional remedies that will correct the base of any number of illnesses; an "...abundance of laughter..."(64a) is one of my favorites!

M5 – The Principle of Metaphysically Arranged: "- coined by Robert Frank; to receive or gain something one has specifically asked for through Visualization or Affirmations but one made no conventional attempts to attain it or purchase it, e.g., two irritant co-workers becoming good friends overnight with neither one making any apologies, (one worker had been repeating "harmony" affirmations), a neighbor giving a color TV to a family she hardly knew because she had too many TV's (mother of family had been visualizing a color TV for her family), a cat crying on the doorstep of a person who had been affirming, "I am free from being alone." [cf. Visualization, End-Result, Visual-Imagery Technique]" (65)

*This is to "...formulate in the mind, a visual picture of the **finished** product or the **finished** accomplishment one desires to manifest in his or her life or another person's life; this visionary picture is held in the mind for a period of time during a visualization exercise, after meditation; expectation of this manifestation is necessary, with no consideration of how it is to happen; e.g., to mentally picture a new red automobile, running smoothly, with yourself as the driver, as opposed to picturing one's self earning the money for the automobile."* (65a)

N1 – The Law of Names: "– Recognition of the name shows knowing the name. To know the complete and true data of a person or psychic skill gives one complete control over the person or psychic skill. Names are associated devices, memory gimmicks, used to remind one of something, both as aspects or descriptions of a phenomenon and as root (germ) sounds. To name a thing structures CONSCIOUSNESS. Naming awakens and expresses in a way the whole brain can know it. [*cf.* LAW OF SIGNATURE, WORDS-WITH-POWER]." (66)

Your name spoken out loud or silently taps into the qualities of you, and each name has a unique vibrational pattern, musical note, color, number value, and meaning.

N2 – The Principle of Negative: "-1. pertains to the pole of polarity that compliments the positive; negative pole is anxious to team with the positive as each supplies what the other lacks; it takes both poles of polarity to make a manifestation in the etheric and Mundane World; passive, static receptive; 2. when used in conjunction with Electricity it means the presence of an excessive amount of electrons in a unit; 3. when used in reference to a worldly experience, it means in poor taste, wrong, bad, harmful, or the opposite of what should have happened according to the morals and belief system of the person making the judgment. [**cf.** Positive, Protons, Negative Thought, Negative Elemental, Law Of Oppositives Appendix 7]" (67)

Sometimes a positive person picks a negative partner to love – or vice-versa – to balance out their own lack of what they perceive as a needed quality, or weakness in themselves.

N3 – The Principle of Negative Stress: "-a psychological response to a situation felt to be inappropriate by the one who makes the response; 1. a feeling of discomfort with one's emotional attitude toward an activity at the time of the activity, and a continual feeling of discomfort until one's point of view regarding the activity is changed; 2. the need for a decision but not having made it; 3. an outside stimuli strong enough to cause strain or distortion in the system for that individual; 4. (Hans Selye) "emotional pressures or suppressed emotions stored in the Nervous System causing an imbalance in the chemicals of the body"; 5. the section of the Sympathetic Nervous System as it increases its right to fire in the flight or fight mechanism. [**cf.** Blocks, Eustress, Negative Thought, Key To Life]" [68]

Negative stress can sometimes work for the benefit of a person when used as a motivational tool to overcome obstacles or to motivate a better performance.

N4 – The Principle of New Birth: "- 1. (ancient philosophies) the graduation of the INITIANT to become an INITIATE; being born into the truth; 2. (current) the rise of an individual to a new plateau in the present incarnation; noticeable by a change in interests, friends, foods, colors, education, vocation, books, and lifestyle. [**cf.** NEW-AGE PSYCHOLOGY, NEW-AGE CONSCIOUSNESS AWARENESS MOVEMENT, PLANETARY WORKER, FUTURISTS]." [69]

You can rise to new heights in your life-time.

N5 – The Law of Non-resistance: "- One can overly desire to accomplish something and keep one's mind and actions on it, constantly. This holds the atoms in rigidity and binds the accomplishment to one because of the strong emotion and activity. One should do one's part as well as one can and then let the plan or situation go, and stop letting it posses one's attention and time; let it unfold and happen; e.g., the little boy plants a tomato seed and, every day, digs it up to see how it is doing, thereby stifling its growth." [70]

Intend something – feel good about it – and then let it go so it can happen.

O1 – The Principle of Objective Dream: "-a dream in which the dream symbol means in the dream what it means in daytime living. [**cf.** Release Type Dreams]" [71]

These symbols sometimes "...release physical and emotional tensions and inner anxiety while the sleeper is having the dream; dreamer awakens feeling much better than the day before..." (71a)

O2 – The Principle of Occult Police: "-highly intelligent Etheric World Intelligences who concern themselves with psychism applied toward criminal ends and offense against society; answerable to anyone who needs help and calls upon them through telepathic communication. [**cf.** White brotherhood, Empathy-PK, Up-For-Grabs, Body Bruises]" (72)

The occult police (also known as "The White Brotherhood") are "...masters that once roamed the earth and are still interested in the earth; white does not mean color of skin, but the state of Evolution (free from spot or blemish and without evil intent)..." (72a)

O3 – The Law of Omnipresence: "- The UNIVERSE is represented in every one of its particles. Everything is made of one- hidden-stuff, TOTALITY, and Totality appears within all its parts; in every grain of sand and star in the sky. It is always present and present everywhere." (73)

A drop of the ocean has all the same elements of the ocean, in using this example you are a drop of totality.

O4 – The Law of One System: " – (new age psychology) There is an intellectual, instinctual psychical and physical link between all living things and a change, small or large, in any one thing promotes a change in all other living things; given tangible evidence by psychic experiments and testing by the KIRLIAN PHOTOGRAPHY, BIOFEEDBACK INSTRUMENTS and PSYCHIC SKILLS. [**cf.** TRANSFORMATION, AQUARIAN AGE]." (74)

You make an impact in the world whether you know it or not.

O5 – The Law of Opposites: "- Everything has a reverse relationship. Anything can be split into two complete reverse characteristics, and each of these reverse characteristics contains the essence of the other in its essence. Each end of polarity contains the potentiality of the elements of the other.   One pole away from a central fixation has its reverse characteristic the same distance or density from the center; eg., positive/negative,   hot/cold,   loud/quiet,   yin/yang,   lingam/yoni, male/female, sick/well, happy/sad, up/down, black/white, stale/fresh. The Slavs have two deities in the etheric world , Byelbog and Chernobog; personifying Darkness and Light, Good and Evil, used together as if both were a part of the one; similar to Christianity's God and Satan. [**cf**. Law of Polarity.]" (75)

You could not experience a positive without a negative with which to compare it.

P1 – The Law of Path: "- What is of worth to one is "his" path, regardless of the hardships it presents, or the length of time it takes. Each individual has a karmic journey which he or she has chosen to pursue in this Incarnation and he will, somehow, find a way to travel on it. This road in one's journey will not go to the individual; he or she will go to it if it proves of worth to them. If it does not, one cannot hold it together successfully in one's dimension of time because it will fall apart of its usefulness. The direction one should take is within each individual, and only that individual can take that road. When one finds their "path" they will constantly have an inner drive to keep on it, and when one is not on it, he or she will feel restless and disturbed. When one finds his "path" one will find security, happiness, and fulfillment from within, regardless of outside circumstances, no matter how traumatic they are. [**cf**. path Symbolism]" (76)

Your instincts will guide you to your purpose in life, but you must first tune in and listen, and then trust them.

P2 - The Law of Personal Transformation: "– (new age psychology) When something new appears in one's life that totally disrupts one's normal lifestyle, one must let go of old patterns, beliefs, mannerisms and activity. The new experience could be an accident, job transference, residential move, new baby, new friendships, a death, etc. The individual should take on a good frame of mind, and eagerly look forward to the new situation; otherwise, his or her growth is held back, the atoms stop flowing and the individual experiences ill health, chaotic activity, and loss of the benefits he or she was to earn from the new lifestyle. The key is to "surrender" and go forth with joy [cf. Holistic Health, Belief System, New-Age Psychology Appendix 5]" (77)

Resisting change inhibits growth.

P3 – The Law of Prosperity: "- Anything less than today's need is not enough. Anything more than today's need is a burden and prosperity lies in between." (78)

The healthy balance between need and greed = prosperity.

P4 – The Principle of Pure Creativity: "-Totality manifesting itself in the physical world through an earth artist; see Inspirational Thought." (79)

"...knowledge or wisdom flows like a stream from the potential within the Human Being Species seed via the Superconscious Mind, to the Right Brain Hemisphere and travels down the Kundalini; information is "pure" or the Truth because it bypasses the subconscious mind and therefore, is not infiltered with one's Belief system..." (79a)

P5 – The Principle of Pyramid Power: "-(Greek *pry,* "fire"; *amid,* "near the center"; "fire in the center") a special condensed energy found inside every Pyramid, made according to the exact scale of the Great Pyramid at Giza; this energy follows the pattern or seed potential of the objects placed within it bringing that person or object closer to its intended perfect state; some items are enhanced and others are preserved when placed within the pyramid form; pyramid must be aligned with one side to the true north; a special condensed energy is found about one/third the way from the bottom that makes changes in animate or inanimate things when placed within the pyramid; energy also emits from the apex of the pyramid; material from which it is made is insignificant as long as it is to exact scale; a framework construction works as well as a solid form; length of time articles should be kept under the pyramid or on top is still in the experimental state. [**cf.** Pyramidology, Forms-With-Power]" (80)

"...shapes that exude energy include the cross, swastika..."(80a), *(before Hitler the swastika was used by a race of Indians as a positive symbol) "...sword, circle, cone, and pyramid; shapes known for protection are the circle and the hexagram..."* (80a)

Q1 – The Principle of QI: "-(China) air or breath; a vital energy in the air necessary for all life; taken into the body by breathing and then broken down into the Yin, negative/feminine and Yang, positive/masculine; see Vital Life Force for details. **Syn.** Life Force, Prana, Biocosmic Energy." (81)

Qi is "...the sum total of Primal Energy from which all mental and physical energy has evolved..."(81a)

Q2 – The Law of Quantum Connection: "-All things, living and non-living, are minutely connected in the ethereal world, and when a physical contact is made and then severed, they will continue to affect one another long after separation, distance being no barrier. Syn. Law of Contagion [**cf.** Radiesthesia, Psychic Healing]" (82)

"...Things, animate or inanimate, once in contact with each other will continue to act upon each other even at a distance, long after the physical contact has been severed. Matter that comes into contact with other matter absorbs or influences that which it contracts..."(82a)

Q3 – The Principle of Quartz: "-(esoteric) a mineral or rock crystal that is hexagonal in form but no two are alike; possesses the property helpful in Dematerialization and rematerialization of a human being; can make the invisible visible and vice versa; capable of being energized from the palm of the hand; used in healing by medicine men and in their rain-making ceremonies; used for Scrying. (Inconcl.) [**cf.** Botane, Alchemy Appendix 2]" (83)

Quartz can be used along with alchemical power, which can be described as "...a science regarding the altering of the structure of an object to another vibrational frequency by mind power and mind control; an art dealing with the control of mutations and transmutations within matter, substance, energy, and life itself, by the mental mind; to change baser metals to gold..."(83a)

Q4 - The Law of Quasi-Immortality: "- Nothing in nature, including man, remains exactly the same for even one second of time. Every time an ATOM changes, everything in the UNIVERSE minutely changes and atoms are constantly vibrating and changing. Atoms travel in cycles and everything follows this cyclic path." (84)

The only thing you can count on in this earth realm is that things are constantly changing, and there is a cyclic time and season for everything.

Q5 – The Principle of Quickened Consciousness: " - The surfacing of stagnant or uneducated energy that is stimulated by a physical experience; outer environmental events frequently occur that at first appear to be negative but result in helping a person express another part of her or himself which they would not have expressed; e.g., the spraining of one's ankle so one will have to stay home from work and read a book that needed reading; cold weather destroying one's flowers, so one has to work in the garden and receive necessary exercise. [**cf.** Expansion Consciousness, Gross Level.]" (85)

Look for and then identify the hidden gift for yourself in every event.

R1 – The Law of Readiness: "- (Eastern) "When the pupil is ready, the Master is ready also; when the student is ready, the Teacher will come." No matter how good a reputation a metaphysical or occult organization has, its only value to you is when the subjects or activities mean something to you, at that "given time." This has nothing to do with the competence or incompetence of the organization or teacher." (86)

The door will open for you when you are ready to walk through it.

R2 – The Law of Reality: "– (esoteric) There is only one Reality, and this is broken down in perception in an infinite number of ways to be viewed in accordance with the number of entities viewing it (on the physical and etheric plane.) Each individual has atoms that have different consciousnesses, a different akashic record, which is being bombarded constantly, but differently, by environmental stimuli. Therefore, the universe, world, countries, weather, prominent people, neighborhoods, animals, plants, communication systems, etc., will be unique to each perceiver, according to his or her current BELIEF SYSTEM (because he knows no other at that time) e.g., this law is obvious when two psychics are given the same message but it is brought through in different symbols. Each person's total belief system makes their consciousness. What one has the consciousness for makes his world and body. This is "real" for him. Reality is function of belief." (87)

People's reality is constructed by their mind – so it is different for every person. (87a)

R3 – The Principle of Rem Rebound Phenomena: "-the Sea Of Faces, (hypnagogic stage), occurring in the middle of the night when an individual is withdrawing from drugs (medicinal or recreational); the repressed dream material and earthbound entities that unconsciously cling to one on drugs, clamor to the surface when one withdraws; the Soul-Mind and Conscious Mind try to set up equilibrium while the patient sleeps, leaving an opening in the Etheric Web; this opening allows the entities and dream material to explode, after their long repression; the sleeper sees grotesque, surrealistic phantoms, and pastiche visions coming rapidly and overcrowding to get in; it is frightening and unpleasant. [**cf.** Hypnagogic State, Earth-Bound Entities, Density]" (88)

Sometimes called a Hypnagogic State, this can also be described as "...a short time span just before sleep takes over, when the conscious and subconscious mind are changing dominancy in their roles; the conscious mind becomes passive and the subconscious mind takes control of the thinking; this process sets up an equilibrium of mind activity and when the two minds are on the same level of activity, there seems to be an unplugging and plugging of circuits in the head; lasts from a few seconds to a few minutes; it goes unnoticed to many; to some, it is a fusing of electrical sparks in the head; to some, a host of energies is perceived clairaudiently as voices and sounds unfamiliar to the sleeper; to others a host of scenes, images, or faces are perceived clairvoyantly and appear grotesque, friendly, unfriendly, pleasant, hazy, vivid, unknown, and seemingly make no sense; as sleep takes over, this disappears from view and memory..."(88a)

Note: During the sixties and seventies they called something like this a "good or bad trip."

R4 – The Principle of Repression: "-to hold back or remove from mental consciousness any experience that is unpleasant and painful, rather than to deal with it at the time it happens; because it is not resolved, it remains painful; as time goes on, other experiences that are remindful of this one, are also shut out or blocked from mental consciousness; these experiences become stored in the body and often result in physical or mental illness. [**cf.** Blocks, Grapes, Clearing, Habits Of Thought]" (89)

Repression causes issues to accumulate like a bunch of grapes. The term "Grapes" is defined as: "...unresolved ideas and concepts which the conscious mind was not in condition to rationalize when formed and are suppressed and stored in the subconscious mind; ideas and concepts unresolved because the emotional content was too much to handle at the time of the experience; as time goes on, emotions of like nature join these, making a larger group which will keep growing until the conscious mind resolves the original experience..."(89a)

R5 – The Law of Ritual: "-Any act performed repeatedly with specific conscious intent becomes a "rite" of that conscious specific intent, whether or not the person is aware of this law. All MATTER used in a customary procedure absorbs and influences the other during that procedure period until it is worn away through another repeated customary procedure; e.g., a kitchen platter absorbs odors of the meat, the attitude of the dishwasher, and the overall atmosphere of the kitchen, with each use. Glasses worn every day are influenced by the characteristics and emotions of the wearer. This is the main law behind PSYCHOMETRY." (90)

Ritual carries with it a great deal of energy, light, force, and impact.

S1 – The Law of Self-knowledge: "– When one is aware of oneself and has information about oneself, and understands these two combinations, one will have complete control over one's behavior, making life pleasurable and joyous. The most important kind of knowledge is knowledge of oneself; "Know Thyself." (91)

All knowledge is but reminding or remembering.

S2 – The Principle of Sensation Consciousness: "-(future science) (botane) an innate ability of the Plant Kingdom to perceive feelings from the emotions , morals, intent, and health of humans, animals, and other plants; these vibrations reach the plant's Aura and affect its growth, color, and length of life. [**cf.** Botane, Anpsi, Minspi, Mandrake, Vegetation Memory]" (92)

When the man I loved broke off our relationship, the beautiful potted orchid he bought me, withered and died less than a week later; I knew at the time is not just a coincidence.

S3 – The Principle of Senses: "-(esoteric) any of the faculties, such as sight, hearing, smell, taste, or touch, designed to co-create objects, situations, relationships, families, jobs, nature, and a place to inhabit; this co-creation is to be used as a school for learning special lessons that are unable to be learned in any other way; as opposed to the theory that the Senses are to give an awareness of the world already created; (Seth) "function of the senses is to create a world, not to permit awareness." [**cf.** New-Age Psychology]" (93)

"...the Mind (subconscious and conscious) has charge of the condition of one's body and the condition of one's daily activity; each person should learn about Thought, Inner-Dialogue, Thought-Forms, emotions and attitudes; if one is concerned with what goes on inside of his or her mind, the outside daily activity will take care of itself; no one is responsible for anyone else but each one is responsible for her or himself and their contribution to the system they live in..." (93a)

S4 - The Law of Suffering: "- (new-age psychology) All misery, agony, or anguish, whether mental or physical, is caused by FEELINGS. These feelings are caused by one's attitude or point of view, regarding what one is experiencing. One's attitude is caused by one's BELIF SYSTEM. The whole range of one's belief system results from earthly thoughts in one's first INCARNATION to the present moment. So, one feels the way one thinks. (94)

You are and experience what you think.

S5 – The Law of Symbolism: "– (Alchemy) Environmental and body happenings are a direct result of one's thinking, emotions, and attitudes, and these outward conditions appear to have much similarity and likeness to these thoughts, emotions, and attitudes. One's body, house, automobile, washing machine, lawn, trees, are an extension of one's self, and an outer symbol of attitudes and emotions; e.g., one who has no money to bank may bank fat on the body as a compensation; the brakes go wrong on the car when one needs to slow down, or one desires to stop something but cannot. [**cf.** HOLISTIC HEALTH, CURATIVE EDUCATION]" (95)

What is kept on the inside shows up on the outside. Look for symbols in your immediate environment that are there to show you what is going on within you.

T1 – The Principle of Tears: "-1. a necessary mechanism in both male and female designed to release stress and to prevent blocks in their systems; has nothing to do with maturity or strength of character; a mechanism to clean out the fears, disappointments, and sadness of one's emotions; 2. (Pir Vilayar Inayat Khan) the waters of the plants of life; an abundance of crying (when necessary) can transform one, as it acts as an alchemical cleanser; 3. white bleeding; tears, allow the hurt to heal from within, similar to red bleeding that cleans out the wound and allows it to heal from within. [**cf.** NEW-AGE PSYCHOLOGY] (96)

Crying is good for your emotional and physical health in that it cleanses you of negative emotions such as fear, resentment, anger, jealousy, etc..

T2 – The Principle of Telluric Energy: "-(esoteric) 1. Magnetism that emanates from the ground and is fed to the human body through the feet; all individuals living on the planet receive this energy which is necessary to sustain the Electricity within the body. **Syn.** Earth Magnetism, Gaus Magnetics. 2. the force that makes the Dowsing Rod pull downward when it has located the sought after underground substance. [**cf.** Forked Stick, L-Rod, Scheme Of Things]" (97)

There is "...an intelligence and/or power that keeps things moving perpetually, with a purpose, and in an orderly fashion; this purpose is greater than one's individual purposes but needs human activities in this orderliness..."(97a)

T3 – The Principle of Therapeutic Touch: "-coined by Delores Krieger; to transfer healing energy from one's hands to the patient to promote normal healing more quickly; to use a special technique to unruffle the energy field of the congested area in the patient; to transfer energy that has been decreed healing in nature, and localized from the hand of the healer to the patient; if the healer has a deep desire to be helpful, the patient's body will show a significant change in the Body Chemistry, especially in the blood cells; the healing energy elicits a generalized relaxation response that puts the patient in a healing mode and the body can heal itself more quickly. Syn. Laying-On-Of-Hands, Magnetic Healing. [**cf.** Powwow, Healing, Nerve Fluid, Passes]" (98)

"...1. The magnetic nerve fluid from the healer's nervous system is transferred from the palms of the hands to the nervous system of the patient; 2. nerve fluid is directed out of the hands to the congested area of the patient, and with special motions the nerve fluid loosens the block in the meridian Lines and the patient starts to heal..."(98a)

T4 – The Law of Thought: "– The mental activity of the HUMAN BEING KINGDOM directs the course of the ATOMS to make third-dimensional manifestations, holds the manifestations in place or frees them, according to his or her needs and desires. (Briefly explained) The mental activity behind the thought sends out ergs of EMOTION and INTELLIGENCE (unstoppable radiations); this emotion and intelligence together start the rate of vibration of electrons and protons in the atoms, according to the nature and emotions behind the thought (emotion has its degrees of voltage). These atoms congregate atoms of like nature to form molecules, molecules form compounds, and compounds form physical matter that mankind can perceive and use for their needs and wants: 1. This explains the cliché "man has dominion over all things"..." (99)

Your thoughts hold your reality, because your world is a product of your thoughts.

T5 – The Law of Threes: "- This begins with two, which is commonly recognized as positive and negative, and becomes law only when it has a neutralizing force. These three then become a unit of themselves, neither of the two becoming more powerful or larger. Now, each behaves for itself and for the benefit of the whole; e.g. Father, Son, HOLY SPIRIT; mother, father, child; CONSCIOUS MIND, SUB-CONSCIOUS MIND, SUPERCONSCIOUS MIND, waking state, sleeping state, dreaming state,; bride, groom, marriage as a unit." (100)

When a positive and a negative force merge (Yin/Yang) there may be a neutralizing effect that produces a third energy form. (100a)

U1 – The Principle of Uncertainty: *"-* (Albert Einstein, Werner Heisenberg) Any realistic description of the universe must describe it in all possible states at the same instant of time; e.g. a person would be alive, dead, and unborn simultaneously, (Inconcl.) [**cf.** TIME DISPLACEMENT, PATTERNING, ACROSS TIME, NO TIME OR SPACE]." (101)

This is to say that the past, present, and future is happening simultaneously. This would explain the feeling of Dejavu.

U2 – The Law of Unfoldment: "- (angel hierarchy) There are seven major phases the SOUL-MIND must experience to purify her or himself to evolve into the divine or the "Godliness". Phases one, two, three, and four, are worked out in the PHYSICAL BODY. Phase five, initiation into Mastership may be earned either in the material plane or ETHERIC PLANE. Phase six, initiation into LORDSHIP is earned in the ETHERIC WORLD. Phase seven, initiation into the unfoldment into Godhood is earned in the higher planes. **Syn. ANGEL EVOLUTION.**" (102)

A moving into a higher state of consciousness can be recognized in a person by a change in one's choices of friends, colors, foods, vocation, behavioral patterns, and attitudes. It can happen suddenly or gradually over time, or through lifetimes.

U3 – The Law of Universal Law: *"-* Principles that are absolutely necessary for this system of universes. All the laws that are necessary were created with CREATION and are existing now, whether mankind has discovered them or not. No other laws will ever be necessary to run the UNIVERSE. These principles have no exception (as do manmade laws) and if events, situations, object, persons, phenomena and Mother Nature act as if an exception to a universal law, it is only because humanity does not understand the law in its entirety. Subordinate and superior laws will govern the exception. **Syn.** NATURAL LAW." (103)

Worth repeating – Universal laws are governed by a higher source. They have no exceptions, and if they seem to, it's only because the law is not understood in its entirety. (103a)

U4 – The Principle of Unripe Egg: "-(Vedic) the part of an individual that is self-centered, arrogant, and materialistic. (104)

This is often a sign of immaturity no matter what the age, or lifetime.

U5 – The Principle of Universal Substance: "-(Jean de Chardin) "the final 'stuff' of the universe is mind stuff"; (Elmer Green) "universe is crystallized thought"; (R. Gammon) "what we know of the world is the structure of the mind"; a system of unheard music; (esoteric) electro-chemical, magnetic vibrations balancing under the law of action and reaction (Karma), forming various levels of energy consciousness which is subject to the law of thought. (Inconcl.) [**cf**. Law Of Thought Appendix 7, Matter, Energy]" (105)

"Everything manifested in earth is the mental equivalent of the thoughts of every man in earth."" (105a)

V1 – The Law of Vibrational Frequencies: "- Everything in the UNIVERSE is vibrating and the rate of vibration determines its nature. There are trillions of vibrational frequencies and each thing, animate and inanimate, is formed, shaped, colored, activity oriented, intelligently endowed, and evolutionary-processed by its entire vibrational frequency and the various frequencies within its unit; e.g. the earth and its products such as steel and iron are slower frequencies than the SEVENTH PLANE and its celestial beings. [**cf**. VIBRATIONS, LAW OF VIBRATION, VIBRATORY NOTE]." (106)

Everything has a certain rate of vibration, and that determines its nature. For example a rapist would have a lower vibration than a nun. You may increase your vibration on our plane of existence by prayer, meditation, affirmations, visualizations, practicing gratitude, treating others as yourself, tithing, deep breathing, right attitude, etc..

V2 – The Law of Vibration: "-Everything in the universe has its foundation in the principle of constant movement and this rate of movement determines its uniqueness and expression. Because of this law, the CONSCIOUS MIND of a person can tune into the SUBCONSCIOUS MIND and UNIVERSAL MIND to receive PSYCHIC INFORMATION. **Syn.** LAW OF QUANTA STATE." (107)

It is like walking into a room and instantly feeling the mood of the crowd. You are tuning in to their collective vibration.

V3 – The Principle of Virgin Spirit: "-Totality, in its original form, divided itself into fractions and ensouled the egos of humans and all other forms of life, causing itself to enter the heavy, imprisoning matter of this world; slowly, patiently, fights its way back to its original virgin state. **Syn.** Totality. [**cf.** Involution, Evolution, Egos]" (108)

"...the decent to a lesser existence with an intent and desire to work upward and return to the chaotic/perfect form..." (108a)

V4 – The Principle of Vital Life Force: "... 10. needed by person's mind to think; taken into the PHYSICAL BODY through the breath and through the chakras, distributed in the bloodstream and the CONSCIOUS MIND and filters into the NERVOUS SYSTEM and SUBCONSCIOUS MIND: utilizes the LAW OF THOUGHT..." (109)

Vital life force cannot be duplicated, destroyed, or made visible. It is the intelligence, energy, and vibrating force in each atom. It is soul and spirit, the universal essence pervading all nature. It is connected with our breathing. There is no barrier to attaining success in some form if you learn how to breathe properly, thereby taking in more vital life force. (109a)

V5 – The Principle of Voluntary Control of Internal States: "-(Elmer Green) "becoming conscious in normal unconscious parts of the body, at will"; ability to turn away from the outside world, enter the Alpha State Of Consciousness or lower, visualize the body feeling in one particular area, and talk to the body mentally to have that area behave as you want it to; most easily attained when Hooked-Up to a Biofeedback Instrument; has proven an aid to healing some diseases. [**cf.** Biofeedback Training, Alpha Mode, Baseline Drift]" (110)

This is "...a state of consciousness in which the body is relaxed, the emotions are quiet, and the mind is controlled..." (110a)

W1 – The Principle of Warming Dream: "-1. a dream that tells the dreamer where he or she stands according to the decisions he or she made that day; this gives the dreamer an option to change plans the next day; 2. a Psychic Experience During Sleep that foretells a mishap in the near future regarding one's self or a loved one, or in the nation. [**cf.** Prophecy]" (111)

The "...information can be warnings, or pleasant news..." (111a)

W2 - The Principle of Wellness: "– a degree of mental and physical HEALTH that one feels comfortable with and tries to maintain; the responsibility for good health and future health rests with one's self; 1. what is good health for one is not necessarily good health for another; a STATE OF CONSCIOUSNESS wherein one can relate to one's self and feel satisfied with one's behavior and lifestyle; good health is not a measurement of one's spiritual growth; how one handles one's wealth is not a method for preventing illness; 2. to balance, resolve, and put in proper perspective the stresses of everyday experiences, without postponing these stresses for future handling, contributes to good health; 3. emphasis should be on a lifestyle that brings harmonious integration of the SOUL-MIND and the CONSCIOUS MIND to bring correct health for the body in this incarnation. [**cf.** NEW-AGE PSYCHOLOGY, CURATIVE EDUCATION, HOLISM]". (112)

"Never put off till tomorrow what you can do today." (112b)

– Thomas Jefferson –

Quotes like these go down in history for a reason! Procrastination can cause negative stress – and negative stress can cause high blood pressure, etc. You are ultimately responsible for your own wellness.

W3 – The Principle of Wheel of Life: "– (Hinduism, Buddhism, Tibet) a circle MANDALA built in three-dimensional form representing mankind's KARMA, resulting in repetitive births, deaths, and rebirths; has three hub outgrowths symbolic of ignorance, lust, and anger; has four spokes symbolic of gods, demigods, tortured souls, and human beings; circle is emblematic of immortality; theory: all people are shackled to the wheel of life and must be reborn in earth until all karma is expended.   [**cf.** PERSONAL LIFE SITUATION, LIFE WAVE]." (113)

(**Dannie Duncan**) "Love is the gravity that holds everything together. When you operate from a center of love (right attitude, and intention with compassion and holding yourself and others as sacred), outwardly - from the inside out - all that you give out will come back to you magnified, resulting in your becoming magnetized (as in Remember). A magnetic personality will give you the ability to draw positive results to yourself. You will be operating under the law of expansion. However, when you operate from a center without love (selfish, or evil attitude, or intention, without compassion or holding yourself and others as sacred) inwardly – from the outside in - you form somewhat of a black hole effect, which results in a demagnetized personality. This ends in all that you want eluding you. In this case, love or gravity will not hold things together (as in Dismember). Things in your life will slowly fall apart on every level (mentally, spiritually, physically, and emotionally). You will be operating under the law of contraction."

Note – *Karma is "Just", but you must* wake up *and* realize that it exists!

W4 – The Principle of White Light: "-(esoteric) the one Energy that contains the energies of all elements and chemicals found in the sun; the basis for all color, being *pure* in its essence; emanations from the Spiritual Sun; represents Totality, the Absolute; the Trinity; white is *pure* love, perfect love is pure and perfect love is all, therefore the white light is All; all is white light and as it extends into the Universe, it is broken up or refracted and one perceives it as color; everything is an extension of the white light; light represents Intelligence; see Totality. [**cf.** Colorology, White, Black]" (114)

The color white is "the perfect blending of all the seven colors of the spectrum making white pure color." "the positive aspect represents good, light, purity, peace, modesty, innocence, gaiety, and happiness..." (114a)

W5 – The Principle of Wisdom: "... 1. strength; there is a strength that comes from knowing; 2. the application of Knowledge; Awareness happens first; practice of awareness turns it into knowledge; the correct and timely use of knowledge turns it into wisdom for that person; this wisdom is then impinged upon the Soul-Mind permanently; e.g., if it is a proper application of a personality trait, one will have that personality trait in every INCARNATION from that time on; whatever the situation was that was handled correctly will not occur again as it is now wisdom and does not have to be reexperienced; wisdom is the correct expression of the potential within the human seed, and once learned, will not have to be handled again; (don juan) "a man of knowledge is one who has followed truthfully the hardships of learning; who has without rushing or without faltering gone as far as he can in unraveling the secrets of personal power." [**cf.** Intelligence]." (115)

Wisdom is when one no longer feels like the observer – but the observer and the observed at the same time. This state results in patience and compassion with all living things.

X1 – The Principle of X-Bio-energies: "- radiations which are given off from people and things and which can be photographed and studied in pictures taken by a high voltage camera; see AURA. (Inconcl.) [**cf.** KIRLIAN EFFECT, ETHERIC DOUBLE]." (116)

This is a colorful Aura radiation given off by people. This electromagnetic field gives energy to your electrical system and serves as a battery for health and vitality. Correct attitude and proper breathing can affect the shape, color, and meaning of this field. (116a)

X2 – The Principle of Xenoglossia: "-1. to spontaneously utter a language that is foreign to one's self during a charismatic religious or evangelistic meeting; occurs when the individual is in an emotional state; theories (a) individual is in a Light Trance state and the foreign utterance is from the subliminal level of the Subconscious Mind; (b) (medieval) a sign that a demon is present; (c) (current) the Holy Spirit has touched the individual and the Holy Spirit is responsible for the utterances; sometimes it comes out in Chanting; three groupings: 1. Neophasia; 2. Linguistic Restitution; 3. true Xenoglossia. **Syn.** Xenglossy. [**cf.** Super Esp, Talking-In-Tongues]" (117)

"…speech can be: an unknown language from another planet, a foreign language from this planet, a change in pitch in chanting, or rapid nonsensical syllables which seem to have no recognizable meaning…" (117a)

X3 - The Principle of X-Factor: "– coined by Colin Wilson (1971); see VITAL LIFE FORCE." (118)

When there is an emotional charge, the atoms in a person may become activated, and then he or she become more magnetic. This is called magnetism. A person with magnetism otherwise known as the X-Factor (sometimes defined as charisma) has a heightened ability to turn thought energy into form or matter (real objects); or the un-manifested in to the manifested.

X4 – The Principle of X-Force: "-1. coined by L.E. Eeman (1947); see Vital Life Force; 2. the energy behind psychic skills. (Inconcl.) [**cf.** Psychic Energy, Force, Third-Eye-Area]" (119)

It is believed that this X-Force (psychic ability - developing the third-eye-area between a person's eyes) is developing "…with increasing speed, for this coming age…" (119a)

X5 – The Principle of X-ness in Space: *"– 1.* an order of neither breadth, length, nor depth, but an order of the FOURTH DIMENSION. (Inconcl.) **2.** the undetermined dimension of the minute pictures of past history of the planet in the astral picture gallery, as seen by good clairvoyants; see MENTAL-REFLECTING-ETHER-(Inconcl.) [**cf.** AKASHIC RECORDS OF THE EARTH, THIRD DIMENSION, SECOND DIMENSION]." (120)

This is a dimension that holds minute pictures of past history of the planet and people in a sort of astral picture gallery. These records utilize the law "for every action there is a reaction," and one finds that he or she makes their new experiences out of their past experiences from these orderly accurate ethereal records. Comparable to a computer it takes in exactly what is fed by the conscious mind and feeds back these records into the bloodstream without being noticed until one reaps outcome in his life. Know that everything you output is input, so be careful and thoughtful. (120a)

Y1 – The Principle of Yang: "– (China) ether that has a positive electrical charge of POLARITY; is active, and has the characteristics of male, sunlight, fire, strength, and heaven; has a complimentary and opposite twin, YIN; found in every element of life with the yin; mutations of YIN AND YANG represent the universal force; in yang is contained the seed of the other. [**cf.** POLARITY Appendix 5]." (121)

This Yang energy constantly seeks to balance with its opposite twin energy Yin and this constant interaction represents the universal force of father/mother divine, or God. Balance is a key to life.

Y2 – The Principle of Ye Are Gods: "– pertains to human beings; theory: God is all; then humanity must be a division of God, or god in a lesser degree; humans have all the attributes of God in a lesser degree. [**cf.** LAW OF REPETITION Appendix 7]." (122)

Just as a drop of the ocean has all the same elements of the ocean in a lesser degree, so humans have all the same attributes of God in a lesser degree, and we are co-creators with the universe.   Everything in the universe is made up of the same energy.

Y3 – The Principle of Yellow: "-one of the primal colors; refers to Christ love, Sunlight, Sun God, or wisdom principle; yellow has the properties for intellectual stimulation and works with the soul-mind in culminating wisdom. [**cf.** Colorology, Red]" (123)

"...color is a strong subtle force shaping human behavior; color has three functions: 1. sensation; a mental and emotional interpretation of what the eye records; each color represents destructive and constructive emotions; 2. chemical; color one wears is infused with the electrical and magnetic qualities of the wearer and attracts to one according to the strength of the color; 3. light." (123a)

Y4 – The Principle of Yellow Diamond: "-(esoteric) a mineral that is influenced by the sun; used as a symbol for the lion and the sun; when worn, brings one courage, leadership and royalty; helps to neutralize the vibrations of the moon. [**cf.** Containers Of Magical Power, Cats Eye]" (124)

"...stones, mountains, rivers, flowers, and all nature contains psychic energy that is attuned to mankind and can be tapped, used, or redirected by the Native American for the benefit of mankind." (124a)

Y5 - The Principle of Yin: "– (China) **1.**   ETHER that has a NEGATIVE electrical charge of POLARITY; found in every element of life with YANG, its complimentary and opposite twin; the mutation of YIN AND YANG represent the universal force; yin is receptive and in yin is contained the seed of the yang; has the characteristics of female, darkness, and represents the moon, weakness, and water. [**cf.** YANG, LINGAM, LINGAM AND YONI, POLARITY Appendix 5]." (125)

This Yin energy constantly seeks to balance with its opposite twin energy Yang and this constant interaction represents the universal force of mother/father divine, or God. Balance is a key to life.

Z1 – The Principle of Zero Point: "– a superior state of AWARENESS where one feels the darkness and silence and yet one is alert to other levels of mind; beneficial in MEDITATION, HYPNOTHERAPY, and PSYCHIC DEVELOPMENT.   [**cf**.   GOING   TO-LEVEL,   ALPHA   STATE   OF CONSCOIUSNESS]" (126)

You can tap into emotional reactions, psychic information, and inspirational thoughts. You can get there by resting, or meditating and becoming less alert to outer stimulation. Tapping into this state has been known to improve all areas of a person's life, especially if done on a regular basis.

Z2 – The Principle of Zoether: "- (root word *zooid*) a thought cell with all attributes of the whole word or theme from which it came; capable of separate movement and of splitting into parts; thought cells acting similar to the zooid. [**cf**. ZOETHIC WAVES, HOLD THE THOUGHT, THOUGHT FORMS, MENTAL PLANE]." (127)

We each create our thoughts. Our thoughts (emotions) change the physiology around us, because of a high degree of electricity or voltage attached to them. Be aware of your habit of thinking and know that you are creating your world with your thoughts. With a new way of thinking you can change your life.

Z3 – The Principle of Zoethic Wave: "– particles of thought in the air, making a universal ETHER, similar to light ether; as one finds electricity in the air, one also finds a more subtle substance comprised of humanity's thoughts; thought connects thought in one gigantic network throughout all ETERNITY; thought or zoethic waves travel at a rate of 250,000 miles per second to their destination; see ATOMS, and LAW OF THOUGHT Appendix 7 for process of thought, **Syn.** LOGOIDAL ETHER. [**cf**. ZOETHER, THOUGHT-FORMS Appendix 5]." (128)

We are similar to a small drop of the ocean still containing all of the same attributes of the whole ocean. We are part of that whole. Our function is to be the part yet draw from the whole. Relax, and let the universe guide you, knowing there is a perfect order behind your life and everything around you. All is as it should be.

Z4 – Principle of Zone of Irritation: "-(radiesthesia) a danger area formed by the crossing of veins of water running underground; this can affect a person who spends much time in the building over the crossing, such as in an area where one sleeps, works, or sits frequently; these zones have been known to cause cancer and other diseases; can be detected by the Dowsing Rod. [**cf.** Dowsing, Dowsing Field]" (129)

The combination of the ..."earth's magnetic field, and the dowsing rod work harmoniously to bring a meaningful answer to a proposed question by the dowser... " (129a)

Z5 – Principle of Zone Therapy: "-a method of healing the body by using compression on the feet with the thumb and fingers; this releases the flow of electrical energy in the nerve endings, which balances the body's Polarity that allows the body cells to normalize and heal themselves. **Syn.** Reflexology. [**cf.** Meridian, Acupuncture Points]" (130)

This technique uses "...twelve, invisible, electrical Nerve Fluid lines in the human body running from the tips of the feet and fingers to the head area connecting all the major organs and glands; these invisible lines have a definite relationship to one's physical health; these body nerve fluid lines behave identical with the universal movements of the sun, earth, moon, and planets..." (130a)

*_{*}*_{*}*

"...live an ordinary but magical life so that every moment, every

person, and everything in it becomes sacred."(131)

– Jeremy Hayward

The hidden wisdom – stay in adventure!

<>*<>*<>*<>*

Dannie Duncan

When I lived in Los Angeles, California, I had to take a city bus every day from West Hollywood to Beverly Hills where I worked as shampoo girl in a hair salon.

One afternoon as I was riding home from work on the Fairfax Boulevard bus, a blind man boarded leading with his walking stick. I immediately began envisioning his sight restored. I closed my eyes and was so into visualizing that I wasn't even aware of anyone around me.

All of a sudden this loud voice went off in my head that shouted, "Get Up and Give Him Your Seat!" The voice was so brash and irritated sounding that it startled me. When I opened my eyes, the blind man was paused in front of me feeling for an open seat with his walking stick.

My face reddened as a wave of embarrassment washed over me. I leaped up to give him my seat, and as I did, several elderly Jewish ladies around me nodded in agreement with my decision to get up. My ego was trying to beckon in a miracle when all this blind man really needed was a seat on the bus.

The hidden wisdom - *small things make a big difference – and are more important than we realize at the time.*

<>*<>*<>*<>*

You attract what you are, and you are what you love!

The hidden wisdom – *choose love in every moment and you will create the life of your dreams!*

<>*<>*<>*<>*

Final note: *I hope you enjoyed the information in this book. I truly believe that it will help in getting you from the ground floor of life, to the first rung of life's ladder. Now - when you are ready to climb to the top of life's ladder, and create the absolutely best, most exciting, mind-boggling life - of your wildest dreams - it is my heart-felt opinion that you: read, watch, or listen to, anything and everything by **Abraham – Hicks Publications**! For a preview go to <u>www.youtube.com</u> ,type in the name Ester Hicks, and watch or listen to as many videos as you can.*

Wishing You Life, Love and Joy,

Dannie Duncan

The beginning!

* * *

References

Front Book Cover –

1) Reproduced with permission from *The Encyclopedic Psychic Dictionary*, by June G. Bletzer, World Tree Press, 401 Thornton Road, Lithia Springs, GA 30122; 770-948-7845 www.newleaf-dist.com. All Rights Reserved, 841.

ii.

1) Joshua David Stone PH.D., *Soul Psychology: How To Clear Negative Emotions And Spiritualize Your Life* (New York: The Ballantine Publishing Group, 1994, 1999, a division of Random House, Inc.), 85.

iv.

1) Lucinda Bassett, *From Panic To Power: Proven Techniques To Calm Your Anxieties, Conquer Your Fears, And Put You In Control Of Your Life* (New York: Collins Wellness; An Imprint of Harper Collins Publishers, 2005), 86.

vi.

1) Charles F. Haanel, *The Master Key System (New York: Barnes & Noble, 2007), 58.*

viii.

1) Louise L. Hay, *You Can Heal Your Life* (California: Hay House, Inc., 1984, 1987, 2004), 114.

Chapter I – Dark Night of the Soul

1) William Collins Sons & Co. Ltd., *Collins English Dictionary* (Complete & Unabridged 10th edition, © Harper Collins Publisher, 1979, 1986, 1998, 2000, 2005, 2006, 2009), http://dictionary.reference.com/browse/nervous%20breakdown .

2) Louise L. Hay, *You Can Heal Your Life* (California: Hay House, Inc., 1984, 1987, 2004), 228.

Chapter II – Mental Healing

1) ***Reproduced with permission from *It's Not Okay Anymore – Your Personal Guide to Ending Abuse, Taking Charge, and Loving Yourself* by Jan Black and Greg Enns. Published by Women's Safety & Resource Center, 1681 Newmark Avenue, Coos Bay, OR 97420. 541-888-1048, 1-888-793-5612. www.womensafety.org <http://www.womensafety.org> All rights reserved. www.inoka.org, 15.

2)   *Reproduced with permission from *The Encyclopedic Psychic Dictionary,* by June G. Bletzer, World Tree Press, 401 Thornton Road, Lithia Springs, GA 30122. 770-948-7845 www.newleaf-dist.com. All Rights Reserved, 837, 845, 847, 849, 679.

3) Dynamic Daily Quotation Website, directory, www.thinkexist.com, Tolerance quotes – The Dalai Lama, http://thinkexist.com/quotation/in_the_practice_of_tolerance-one-s_enemy_is_the/145381.html

 4) Joshua David Stone PH.D., *Soul Psychology: How To Clear Negative Emotions And Spiritualize Your Life* (New York: The Ballantine Publishing Group, 1994, 1999, a division of Random House, Inc.), 160- 162.

5) Louise L. Hay, *Empowering Women: Every Woman's Guide to Successful Living* (California: Hay House, Inc., 1997 and New York: Hay House Inc., 1997), 84.

6-7) Dr. Wayne W. Dyer, *The Power of Intention: Learning to Co-create Your World Your Way* (California: Hay House, Inc., 2004), 250, 256.

8) Charles F. Haanel, *The Master Key System* (New York: Barnes & Noble, Inc., 2007), 86.

9) Louise Hay and Cheryl Richardson, *You Can Create an Exceptional Life* (California: Hay House, Inc., 2011), 30.

10) Lucinda Bassett, *From Panic To Power: Proven Techniques To Calm Your Anxieties, Conquer Your Fears, And Put You In Control Of Your Life* (New York: Collins Wellness; An Imprint of Harper Collins Publishers, 2005), 143.

11) Terry Cole-Whittaker, *What You Think Of Me Is None of My Business* (California: Oak Tree Publications, 1979, and New York: Jove Books by The Berkeley Publishing Group, 1988), 186.

12) Caroline Myss PH.D., *Anatomy of the Spirit: The Seven Stages of Power And Healing* (New York: Three Rivers Press, 1996), 182.

Chapter III – Breakdown

Part I: Breakdown – Sex Addicts

1) William Collins Sons & Co. Ltd., *Collins English Dictionary* (Complete & Unabridged 10th edition, © Harper Collins Publisher, 1979, 1986, 1998, 2000, 2005, 2006, 2009),
http://dictionary.reference.com/browse/reaction+formation?s=t

Part II – Breakdown Gamblers

****

Part III – Breakdown - Alcoholics

1) Dawn Masler, *The Broken Picker Fixer, From Heartbreak to Soulmate: Finding the Love You Deserve in 12 Weeks or Less* (Florida: Abundance Books, 2009), 3.

2) *Reproduced with permission from *The Encyclopedic Psychic Dictionary,* by June G. Bletzer, World Tree Press, 401 Thornton Road, Lithia Springs, GA 30122. 770-948-7845 www.newleaf-dist.com. All Rights Reserved, 59.

Chapter IV – Emotional Healing

1& 2) ***Reproduced with permission from *It's Not Okay Anymore – Your Personal Guide to Ending Abuse, Taking Charge, and Loving Yourself* by Jan Black ands Greg Enns. Published by Women's Safety & Resource Center, 1681 Newmark Avenue, Coos Bay, OR 97420. 541-888-1048, 1-888-793-5612. www.womensafety.org <http://www.womensafety.org> All rights reserved. www.inoka.org, 14, 15.

3) *Reproduced with permission from *The Encyclopedic Psychic Dictionary,* by June G. Bletzer, World Tree Press, 401 Thornton Road, Lithia Springs, GA 30122. 770-948-7845 www.newleaf-dist.com. All Rights Reserved, 522, 685, 838, 841, 845, 848- 849, 852, 854.

4) Bro. Art Renz & Sister Sue, Global Missionary Church Ministries, "A website with religious texts," www.hissheep.com, "Take Every Thought Captive," Outline by Bro. Art Renz & Sister Sue, http://www.hissheep.org/deliverance/taking_every_thought_captive.html

5) Online Parallel Bible Project, "Search, read, study, the bible in many languages," www.biblos.com, "Romans 8:28," **http://bible.cc/romans/8-28.htm**

6) * Joshua David Stone PH.D., *Soul Psychology: How To Clear Negative Emotions And Spiritualize Your Life* (New York: The Ballantine Publishing Group, 1994, 1999, a division of Random House, Inc.), 159-162.

7) Terry Cole-Whittaker, *What You Think Of Me Is None of My Business* (California: Oak Tree Publications, 1979, and New York: Jove Books by The Berkeley Publishing Group, 1988), 186.

8) Online Parallel Bible Project, "Search, read, study, the bible in many languages," www.biblos.com, "Mark 3:25," http://bible.cc/mark/3-25.htm

9) Maya Angelou, *Letter to My Daughter* (New York: Random House, 2008), 108.

10) Eckhart Tolle, *A New Earth* (New York: Plume, Published by Penguin Group, 2005), 105.

11) Deepak Chopra, *How to Know God: The Soul's Journey into the Mystery of Mysteries* (New York: Harmony Books, 2000), 172.

12) Terry Cole-Whittaker, *What You Think Of Me Is None of My Business* (California: Oak Tree Publications, 1979, and New York: Jove Books by The Berkeley Publishing Group, 1988), 186.

13) Robin McGraw, *Inside My Heart, Choosing To Live With Passion And Purpose* (Tennessee: Nelson Books, A Division of Thomas Nelson Publishers, 2006), 141.

14) Louise L. Hay, *You Can Heal Your Life* (California: Hay House, Inc., 1984, 1987, 2004), 34.

Chapter V – Warriors Don't Carry Baggage

****

Chapter VI – Physical Healing

1) ***Reproduced with permission from *It's Not Okay Anymore – Your Personal Guide to Ending Abuse, Taking Charge, and Loving Yourself* by Jan Black ands Greg Enns. Published by Women's Safety & Resource Center, 1681 Newmark Avenue, Coos Bay, OR 97420. 541-888-1048, 1-888-793-5612. www.womensafety.org <http://www.womensafety.org> All rights reserved. www.inoka.org, 16.

2) *Reproduced with permission from *The Encyclopedic Psychic Dictionary,* by June G. Bletzer, World Tree Press, 401 Thornton Road, Lithia Springs, GA 30122. 770-948-7845 www.newleaf-dist.com. All Rights Reserved, 618, 846, 849-851.

3) *Joshua David Stone PH.D., *Soul Psychology: How To Clear Negative Emotions And Spiritualize Your Life* (New York: The Ballantine Publishing Group, 1994, 1999, a division of Random House, Inc.), 161-162, 164.

4) Eckhart Tolle, *A New Earth* (New York: Plume, Published by Penguin Group, 2005), 224.

5) Online Parallel Bible Project, "Search, read, study, the bible in many languages," www.biblos.com, "Proverbs 16:18," http://bible.cc/proverbs/16-18.htm

6) Online Parallel Bible Project, "Search, read, study, the bible in many languages," www.biblos.com, "Isaiah 1:18," http://bible.cc/isaiah/1-18.htm

7) Dr. Phillip C. McGraw, Ph.D., *Life Strategies: Doing What Works Doing What matters* (New York: Hyperion, 1999), 211.

8) Eckhart Tolle, *The Power of Now: A Guide to Spiritual Enlightenment* (California: New World Library, 1999), 222.

9) Jeremy Hayward, *Sacred World: A Guide to Shambhala Warriorship in Daily Life* (New York: A Bantam Book, 1995), 60.

10) New Christian Church of Full Endeavor, Ltd., *A Course in Miracles, The Text, The Workbook, The Manual For Teachers* (Wisconsin: The Advent Of A Great Awakening and a Course In Miracles International Imprints of Endeavor Academy New Christian Church of Full Endeavor, Ltd., 2005), 1022.

Chapter VII – Ida Duke

1) *Reproduced with permission from *The Encyclopedic Psychic Dictionary,* by June G. Bletzer, World Tree Press, 401 Thornton Road, Lithia Springs, GA 30122. 770-948-7845 www.newleaf-dist.com. All Rights Reserved, 838

Chapter VIII – Spiritual Healing

1) ***Reproduced with permission from *It's Not Okay Anymore – Your Personal Guide to Ending Abuse, Taking Charge, and Loving Yourself* by Jan Black ands Greg Enns. Published by Women's Safety & Resource Center, 1681 Newmark Avenue, Coos Bay, OR 97420. 541-888-1048, 1-888-793-5612. www.womensafety.org <http://www.womensafety.org> All rights reserved. www.inoka.org, 16.

2) *Reproduced with permission from *The Encyclopedic Psychic Dictionary,* by June G. Bletzer, World Tree Press, 401 Thornton Road, Lithia Springs, GA 30122. 770-948-7845 www.newleaf-dist.com. All Rights Reserved, 842-843, 845, 847-848.

3) A readers and book recommendations website, Otis Chandler – founder & CEO of Goodreads inc.. Goodreads.com, "When you know better you do better." — Maya Angelou, http://www.goodreads.com/quotes/search?q=when+you+know+better +you+do+better

4) *Joshua David Stone PH.D., *Soul Psychology: How To Clear Negative Emotions And Spiritualize Your Life* (New York: The Ballantine Publishing Group, 1994, 1999, a division of Random House, Inc.), 160-162.

5-6) Dr. Phillip C. McGraw, Ph.D., *Life Strategies: Doing What Works Doing What Matters* (New York: Hyperion, 1999), 109, 184.

7) Bill Walz, "Not Two, One" Rapid River Magazine, April 2009, https://billwalz.com/Not_Two__One.html (accessed January 27, 2012)

8) Iyanla Vanzant, *In the Meantime: Finding Yourself and the Love You Want* (New York: A Fireside Book, Published by Simon & Shuster, 1999), 114.

9) New Christian Church of Full Endeavor, Ltd., *A Course in Miracles, The Text, The Workbook, The Manual For Teachers* (Wisconsin: The Advent Of A Great Awakening and a Course In Miracles International Imprints of Endeavor Academy New Christian Church of Full Endeavor, Ltd., 2005), 430.

10) A readers and book recommendations website, Otis Chandler – founder & CEO of Goodreads inc.. Goodreads.com, "Men feel cherished when they are needed, Women feel cherished when they are loved." — John Gray, **http://www.goodreads.com/author/quotes/848**

11) Esther and Jerry Hicks, *Ask and it is Given: Learning to Manifest Your Desires* (California: Hay House, Inc., 2004), 73.

Chapter IX – Become Your Own Hero

1) Victor E. Frankl, *Mans's Search for Meaning* (New York: Pocket Books, A Division of Simon & Schuster, Inc., 1985), 175.

2-3) Jeremy Hayward, *Sacred World: A Guide to Shambhala Warriorship in Daily Life* (New York: A Bantam Book, 1995), 161.

Chapter X – As Within, So Without

1) A positive and uplifting information website, Scott Mowry and Dan Rezac - website owners, http://www.miraclesandinspiration.com, Eckhart Tolle – Raising Consciousness to Inspire Human Evolution, Part 2: Eckhart Tolle Quotes, "...you don't live your life, but life lives you. Life is the dancer and you are the dance." — Eckhart Tolle, http://www.miraclesandinspiration.com/eckharttolle_quotes.html

2) Eckhart Tolle, *The Power of Now: A Guide to Spiritual Enlightenment* (California: New World Library, 1999).

3) UCLA Kidney Cancer program, a site "...about the Kidney Cancer Program at UCLA in Los Angeles, California," www.kidneycancer.ucla.edu, "Good health is a crown on a well man's head that only a sick man can see," http://kidneycancer.ucla.edu/body.cfm?id=26

Chapter XI – Happily Ever After is a State of Mind

1 - 2) Reproduced with permission from *The Encyclopedic Psychic Dictionary,* by June G. Bletzer, World Tree Press, 401 Thornton Road , Lithia Springs , GA 30122 . 770-948-7845 www.newleaf-dist.com. All Rights Reserved, 837, 847.

3) Online Parallel Bible Project, "Search, read, study, the bible in many languages," www.biblos.com, "JOB 3:25," http://bible.cc/job/3-25.htm

4) An internet news site, www.NaturalNews.com, Real news powered by the people, naturally. Water and positive thoughts - Increase the life-giving properties of this vital resource, Saturday, June 04, 2011 by: Richard Stossel, http://www.naturalnews.com/032604_water_structure.html

5) Anita Moorjani, *Dying To Be Me* (Carlsbad, California and New York City: Hay House, Inc., 2012), 183.

6) An internet movie database site, IMDb Inc., www.imdb.com, "A Synopsis for The Wizard of Oz ," , http://www.imdb.com/title/tt0032138/synopsis

Chapter XII – An expanded Glossary of: Universal Laws and Principles

1- 40) Reproduced with permission from *The Encyclopedic Psychic Dictionary,* by June G. Bletzer, World Tree Press, 401 Thornton Road , Lithia Springs , GA 30122 . 770-948-7845 www.newleaf-dist.com. All

Lithia Springs, GA 30122. 770-948-7845 www.newleaf-dist.com. All Rights Reserved, 224.

64a-65a) Reproduced with permission from *The Encyclopedic Psychic Dictionary,* by June G. Bletzer, World Tree Press, 401 Thornton Road, Lithia Springs, GA 30122. 770-948-7845 www.newleaf-dist.com. All Rights Reserved, 18, 204.

71a-72a) Reproduced with permission from *The Encyclopedic Psychic Dictionary,* by June G. Bletzer, World Tree Press, 401 Thornton Road, Lithia Springs, GA 30122. 770-948-7845 www.newleaf-dist.com. All Rights Reserved, 531, 681.

79a-80a) Reproduced with permission from *The Encyclopedic Psychic Dictionary,* by June G. Bletzer, World Tree Press, 401 Thornton Road, Lithia Springs, GA 30122. 770-948-7845 www.newleaf-dist.com. All Rights Reserved, 242, 317.

81-130) Reproduced with permission from *The Encyclopedic Psychic Dictionary,* by June G. Bletzer, World Tree Press, 401 Thornton Road , Lithia Springs , GA 30122 . 770-948-7845 www.newleaf-dist.com. All Rights Reserved, 521-522, 532, 553, 618, 622, 625, 658-659, 667, 669-670, 672, 676-677, 679-681, 685, 691, 693-694, 852, 854-856.

81a-83a) Reproduced with permission from *The Encyclopedic Psychic Dictionary,* by June G. Bletzer, World Tree Press, 401 Thornton Road, Lithia Springs, GA 30122. 770-948-7845 www.newleaf-dist.com. All Rights Reserved, 14, 483, 840.

87a-89a) Reproduced with permission from *The Encyclopedic Psychic Dictionary,* by June G. Bletzer, World Tree Press, 401 Thornton Road, Lithia Springs, GA 30122. 770-948-7845 www.newleaf-dist.com. All Rights Reserved, 259, 295, 852.

93a) Reproduced with permission from *The Encyclopedic Psychic Dictionary,* by June G. Bletzer, World Tree Press, 401 Thornton Road, Lithia Springs, GA 30122. 770-948-7845 www.newleaf-dist.com. All Rights Reserved, 428.

97a-98a) Reproduced with permission from *The Encyclopedic Psychic Dictionary,* by June G. Bletzer, World Tree Press, 401 Thornton Road, Lithia Springs, GA 30122. 770-948-7845 www.newleaf-dist.com. All Rights Reserved, 369, 543.

100a) Reproduced with permission from *The Encyclopedic Psychic Dictionary,* by June G. Bletzer, World Tree Press, 401 Thornton Road, Lithia Springs, GA 30122. 770-948-7845 www.newleaf-dist.com. All Rights Reserved, 855.

103a) Reproduced with permission from *The Encyclopedic Psychic Dictionary,* by June G. Bletzer, World Tree Press, 401 Thornton Road, Lithia Springs, GA 30122. 770-948-7845 www.newleaf-dist.com. All Rights Reserved, 856.

105a) Reproduced with permission from *The Encyclopedic Psychic Dictionary,* by June G. Bletzer, World Tree Press, 401 Thornton Road, Lithia Springs, GA 30122. 770-948-7845 www.newleaf-dist.com. All Rights Reserved, 855.

108a-110a) Reproduced with permission from *The Encyclopedic Psychic Dictionary,* by June G. Bletzer, World Tree Press, 401 Thornton Road, Lithia Springs, GA 30122. 770-948-7845 www.newleaf-dist.com. All Rights Reserved, 16, 325, 670, .

111a) Reproduced with permission from *The Encyclopedic Psychic Dictionary,* by June G. Bletzer, World Tree Press, 401 Thornton Road, Lithia Springs, GA 30122. 770-948-7845 www.newleaf-dist.com. All Rights Reserved, 676, 677.

112b) A quotation website, BookRags Media Network, www.brainyquote.com, Thomas Jefferson Quotes – "Never put off till tomorrow what you can do today" http://www.brainyquote.com/quotes/quotes/t/thomasjeff16389 1.html

114a) Reproduced with permission from *The Encyclopedic Psychic Dictionary,* by June G. Bletzer, World Tree Press, 401 Thornton Road,

Lithia Springs, GA 30122. 770-948-7845 www.newleaf-dist.com.   All
Rights Reserved, 681.

116a-117a) Reproduced with permission from *The Encyclopedic Psychic Dictionary*, by June G. Bletzer, World Tree Press, 401 Thornton Road, Lithia Springs, GA 30122. 770-948-7845 www.newleaf-dist.com.   All Rights Reserved, 52, 614.

119a-120a) Reproduced with permission from *The Encyclopedic Psychic Dictionary*, by June G. Bletzer, World Tree Press, 401 Thornton Road, Lithia Springs, GA 30122. 770-948-7845 www.newleaf-dist.com.   All Rights Reserved, 12, 628.

123a-124a) Reproduced with permission from *The Encyclopedic Psychic Dictionary*, by June G. Bletzer, World Tree Press, 401 Thornton Road, Lithia Springs, GA 30122. 770-948-7845 www.newleaf-dist.com.   All Rights Reserved, 122, 132.

129a-130a) Reproduced with permission from *The Encyclopedic Psychic Dictionary*, by June G. Bletzer, World Tree Press, 401 Thornton Road, Lithia Springs, GA 30122. 770-948-7845 www.newleaf-dist.com.   All Rights Reserved, 177, 396.

131) Jeremy Hayward, *Sacred World: A Guide to Shambhala Warriorship in Daily Life* (New York: A Bantam Book, 1995), 228.

Contact Info

We'd like to hear your story and, or how this book may have positively impacted your life. To leave feedback for the author - **Email***: dannieduncan@yahoo.com.*

$$*_*\!*_*\!*$$

Adventure into Aging

On the Wings of Time!

$$*_*\!*_*\!*$$

Don't Hold on to Anything too Tightly, or You'll Lose it!

$*_**_**$

..*

Stay Young by Moving Forward!

..*

Your Sense of Humor Will Carry You Through Life!

Remember to laugh and be happy!

Made in the USA
Coppell, TX
17 March 2023

14374728R00142